JOSEPH HAYDN

DIE SCHÖPFUNG
THE CREATION

Oratorium für Solostimmen, Chor und Orchester
Oratorio for Solo Voices, Choir and Orchestra

Hob. XXI: 2

Neuausgabe von / New Edition by
Klaus Burmeister

Klavierauszug vom Herausgeber
auf der Grundlage des von Haydn autorisierten Klavierauszuges
von August Eberhard Müller (1800)

Piano reduction by the editor
based on the piano reduction by August Eberhard Müller (1800),
authorized by Haydn

EIGENTUM DES VERLEGERS · ALLE RECHTE VORBEHALTEN
ALL RIGHTS RESERVED

C. F. PETERS

FRANKFURT/M. · LEIPZIG · LONDON · NEW YORK

DIE SCHÖPFUNG / THE CREATION

Oratorium für drei Solostimmen, Chor und Orchester von Joseph Haydn

Text nach John Miltons Epos „Paradise Lost", deutsche Übersetzung von Gottfried van Swieten. Fertiggestellt 1798; erste öffentliche Aufführung am 19. März 1799 im Burgtheater Wien.

Oratorio for three solo voices, choir and orchestra by Joseph Haydn

Words after Milton's epic poem "Paradise Lost", translated into German by Gottfried van Swieten. Completed 1798. First public performance on 19 March 1799 at the Burg Theater in Vienna.

Soli:
Sopran (Gabriel, Eva) · Tenor (Uriel) · Bass (Raphael, Adam)
Alt (Schlusschor, Nr. 35)

INHALT / CONTENTS

Teil I / Part I

1. OUVERTURE 1
   (Die Vorstellung des Chaos)
   (The Representation of Chaos)

2. REZITATIV (Raphael) und CHOR 3
   Im Anfange schuf Gott Himmel und Erde
   In the beginning God created the heaven and the earth

3. ARIE (Uriel) und CHOR 6
   Nun schwanden vor dem heiligen Strahle
   Now vanish before the holy beams

4. REZITATIV (Raphael) 20
   Und Gott machte das Firmament
   And God made the firmament

5. SOLO (Gabriel) mit CHOR 22
   Mit Staunen sieht das Wunderwerk
   The marv'llous work beholds amaz'd

6. REZITATIV (Raphael) 28
   Und Gott sprach: Es sammle sich das Wasser
   And God said: Let the waters under the heaven be

7. ARIE (Raphael) 29
   Rollend in schäumenden Wellen
   Rolling in foaming billows

8. REZITATIV (Gabriel) 36
   Und Gott sprach: Es bringe die Erde Gras hervor
   And God said: Let the earth bring forth grass

9. ARIE (Gabriel) 37
   Nun beut die Flur das frische Grün
   With verdure clad the fields appear

10. REZITATIV (Uriel) 42
    Und die himmlischen Heerscharen
    And the heavenly host proclaimed

11. CHOR 43
    Stimmt an die Saiten, ergreift die Leier!
    Awake the harp, the lyre awake!

12. REZITATIV (Uriel) 52
    Und Gott sprach: Es sei'n Lichter
    And God said: Let there be lights in the firmament

13. REZITATIV (Uriel) 53
    In vollem Glanze steiget jetzt die Sonne
    In splendor bright is rising now the sun

14. CHOR mit SOLI 56
    Die Himmel erzählen die Ehre Gottes
    The heavens are telling the glory of God

Teil II / Part II

15. REZITATIV (Gabriel) 74
    Und Gott sprach: Es bringe das Wasser
    And God said: Let the waters bring forth

16. ARIE (Gabriel) 75
    Auf starkem Fittiche schwinget sich der Adler
    On mighty pens uplifted soars the eagle

17. REZITATIV (Raphael) 84
    Und Gott schuf große Walfische
    And God created great whales

18. REZITATIV (Raphael) 86
    Und die Engel rührten ihr' unsterblichen Harfen
    And the angels struck their immortal harps

19. TERZETT (Gabriel, Uriel, Raphael) 86
    In holder Anmut steh'n, mit jungem Grün
    Most beautiful appear, with verdure young

20. TERZETT (Gabriel, Uriel, Raphael) und CHOR 94
    Der Herr ist groß in seiner Macht
    The Lord is great, and great his might

21. REZITATIV (Raphael) 111
    Und Gott sprach: Es bringe die Erde hervor
    And God said: Let the earth bring forth

22. REZITATIV (Raphael) 111
    Gleich öffnet sich der Erde Schoß
    Straight opening her fertile womb

23. ARIE (Raphael) 115
    Nun scheint im vollem Glanze der Himmel
    Now heav'n in fullest glory shone

24. REZITATIV (Uriel) 120
    Und Gott schuf den Menschen
    And God created man in his own image

25. ARIE (Uriel) 121
    Mit Würd' und Hoheit angetan
    In native worth and honour clad

26. REZITATIV (Raphael) 126
    Und Gott sah jedes Ding
    And God saw ev'rything

27. CHOR 127
    Vollendet ist das große Werk (I)
    Achieved is the glorious work (I)

28. TERZETT (Gabriel, Uriel, Raphael) 132
    Zu dir, o Herr, blickt alles auf
    On thee each living soul awaits

29. CHOR 140
    Vollendet ist das große Werk (II)
    Achieved is the glorious work (II)

Teil III / Part III

30. REZITATIV (Uriel) 150
    Aus Rosenwolken bricht
    In rosy mantle appears

31. DUETT (Eva, Adam) und CHOR 154
    Von deiner Güt', o Herr und Gott
    By thee with bliss, O bounteous Lord

32. REZITATIV (Adam, Eva) 184
    Nun ist die erste Pflicht erfüllt
    Our duty we performed now

33. DUETT (Adam, Eva) 187
    Holde Gattin! Dir zur Seite
    Graceful consort! At thy side

34. REZITATIV (Uriel) 203
    O glücklich Paar, und glücklich immerfort
    O happy pair, and always happy yet

35. CHOR mit SOLI 204
    Singt dem Herren alle Stimmen!
    Sing the Lord, ye voices all!

Nachwort / Afterword 218

BESETZUNG / ORCHESTRATION

3 Flauti – 2 Oboi – 2 Clarinetti – 2 Fagotti – Contrafagotto
2 Corni – 2 Clarini – 3 Tromboni – Timpani
Violino I – Violino II – Viola – Violoncello – Contrabbasso – Cembalo
Soli: Soprano – Alto (No. 35) – Tenore – Basso
Coro

Aufführungsdauer / Duration: ca. 105 Min.

Partitur / Full Score EP 8997
Aufführungsmaterial leihweise und käuflich erhältlich
Orchestral material is available for hire and purchase

DIE SCHÖPFUNG · THE CREATION

Teil I · Part I

Nr. 1 Ouverture · No. 1 Overture
Die Vorstellung des Chaos · The Representation of Chaos

Joseph Haydn (1732-1809)
Hob. XXI: 2
Herausgegeben von / Edited by Klaus Burmeister

Edition Peters Nr. 8998   32243   © 2002 by C. F. Peters

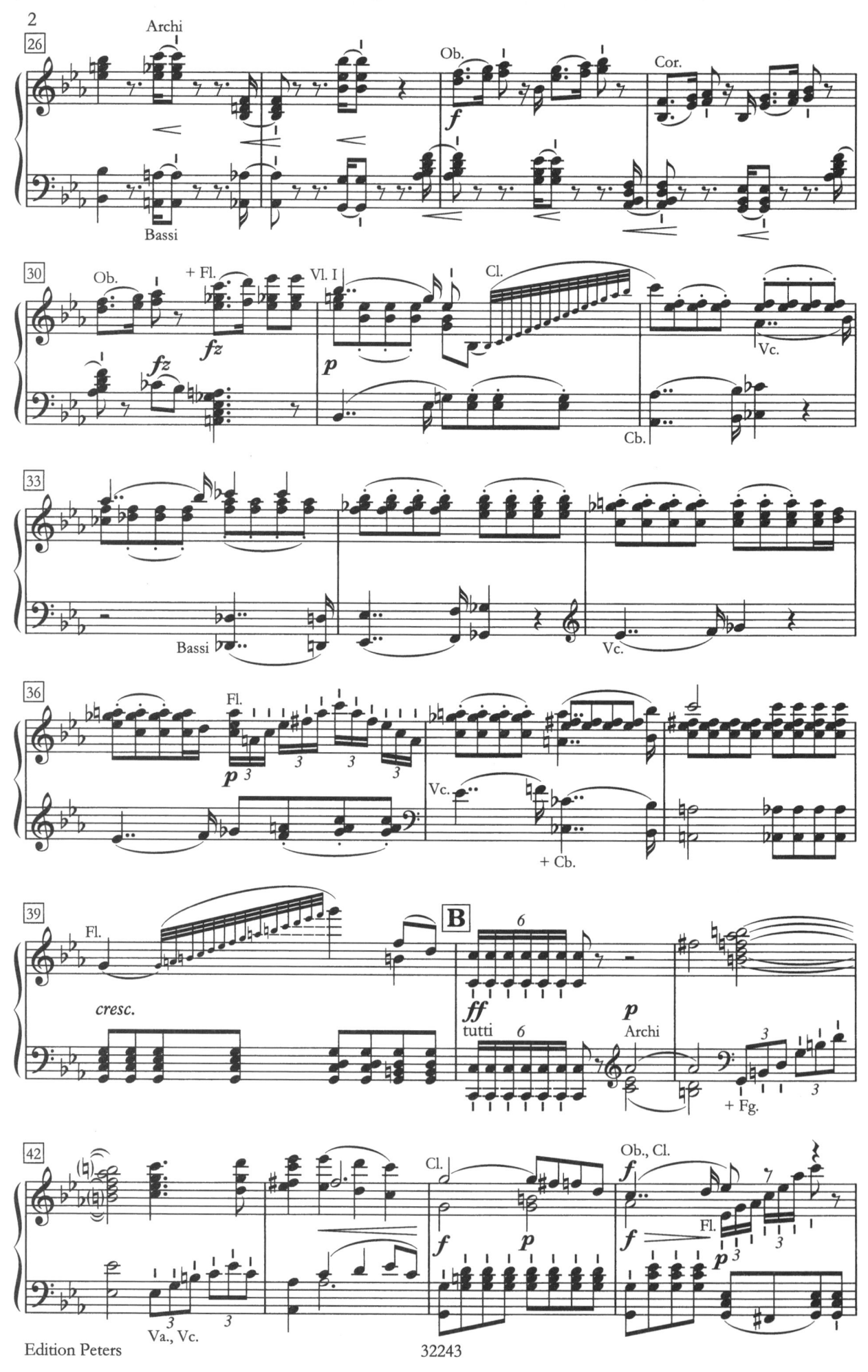

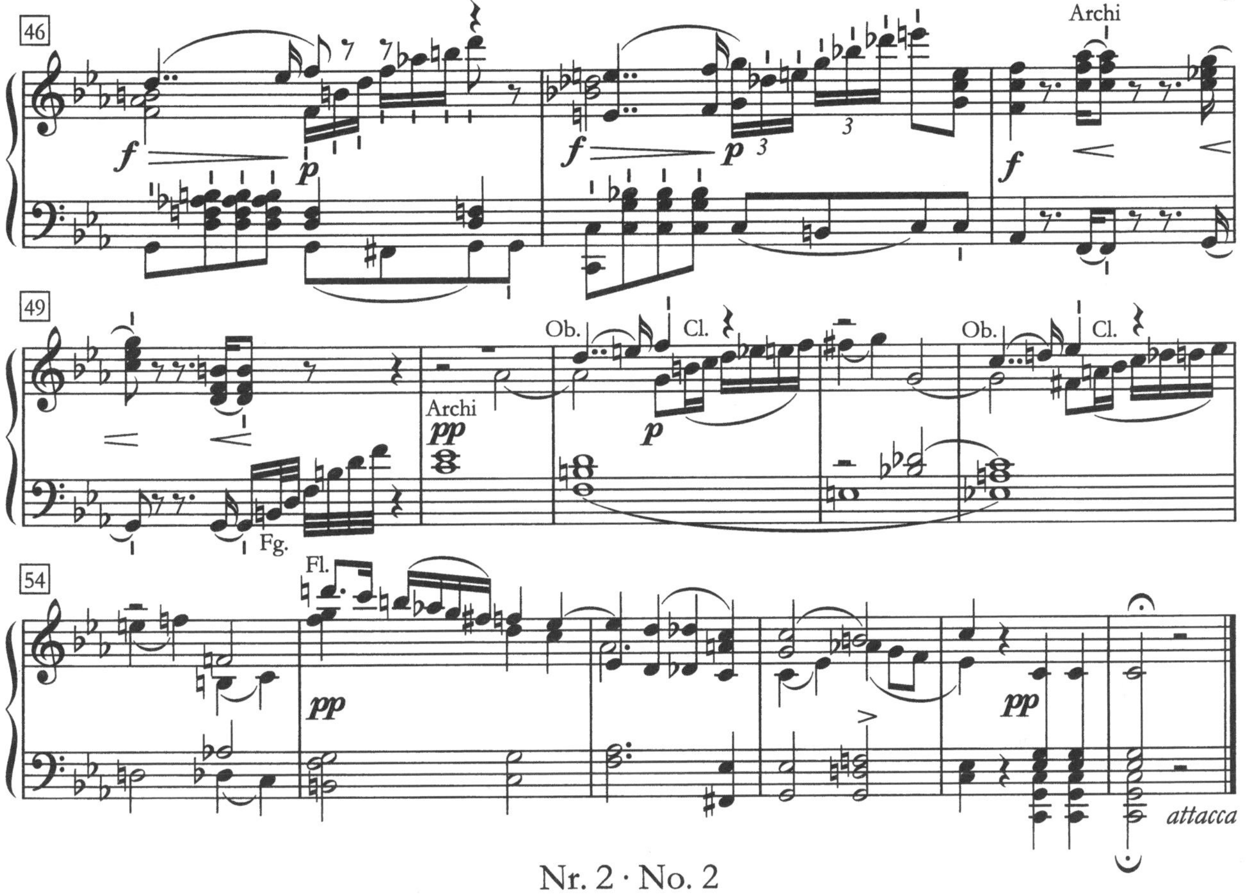
46
Archi
49
Ob.
Cl.
Archi
Ob.
Cl.
Fg.
54
Fl.
attacca

Nr. 2 · No. 2

Rezitativ und Chor · Recitative and Chorus

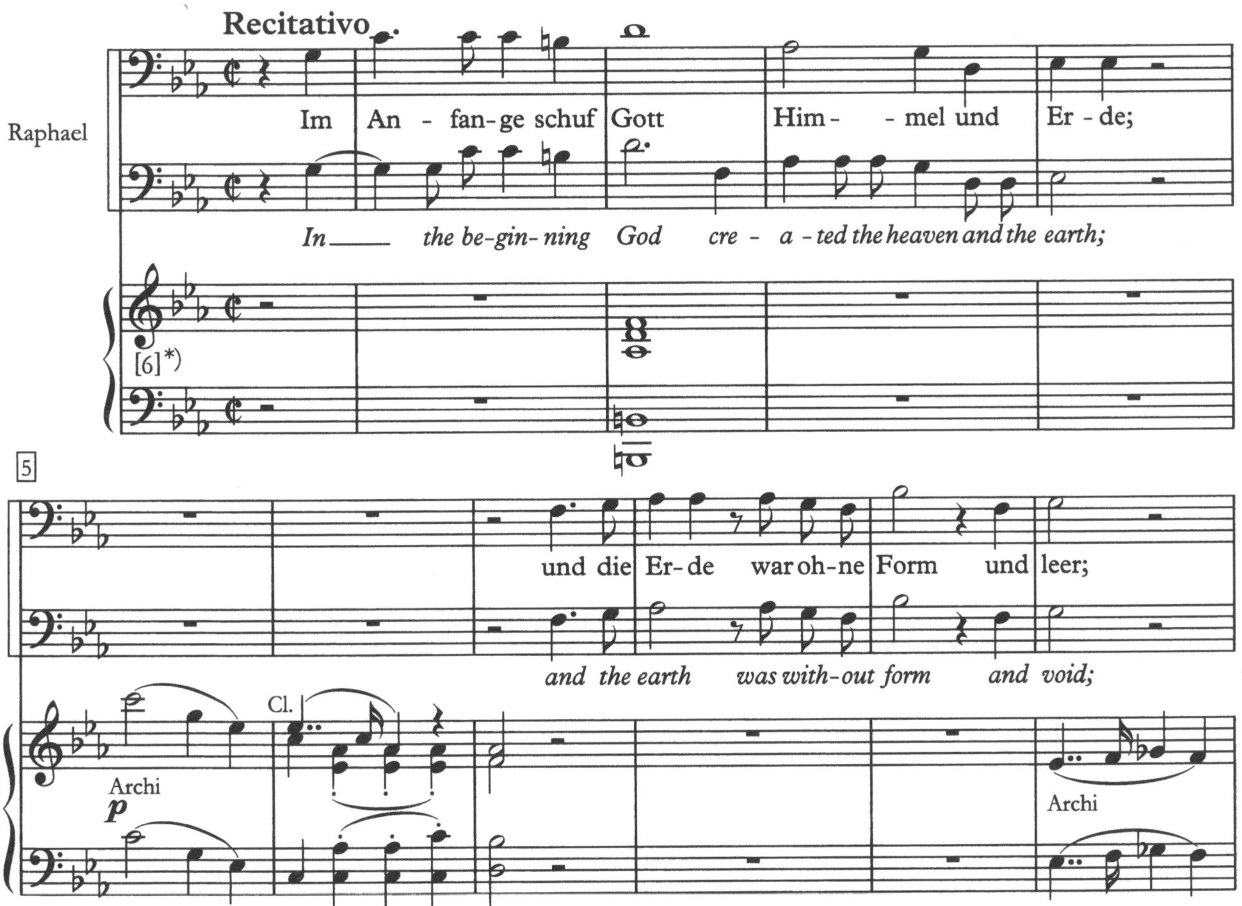
Recitativo
Raphael
Im An - fan-ge schuf Gott Him - - mel und Er - de;
In ___ *the be-gin-ning God cre - a - ted the heaven and the earth;*
[6]*)
5
und die Er-de war oh-ne Form und leer;
and the earth was with-out form and void;
Archi
Cl.
Archi

*) Ziffern in eckigen Klammern verweisen auf die Seitenzahlen des älteren Klavierauszugs Edition Peters Nr. 66.
The numbers in square brackets refer to the page numbering of the old vocal score Edition Peters No. 66.

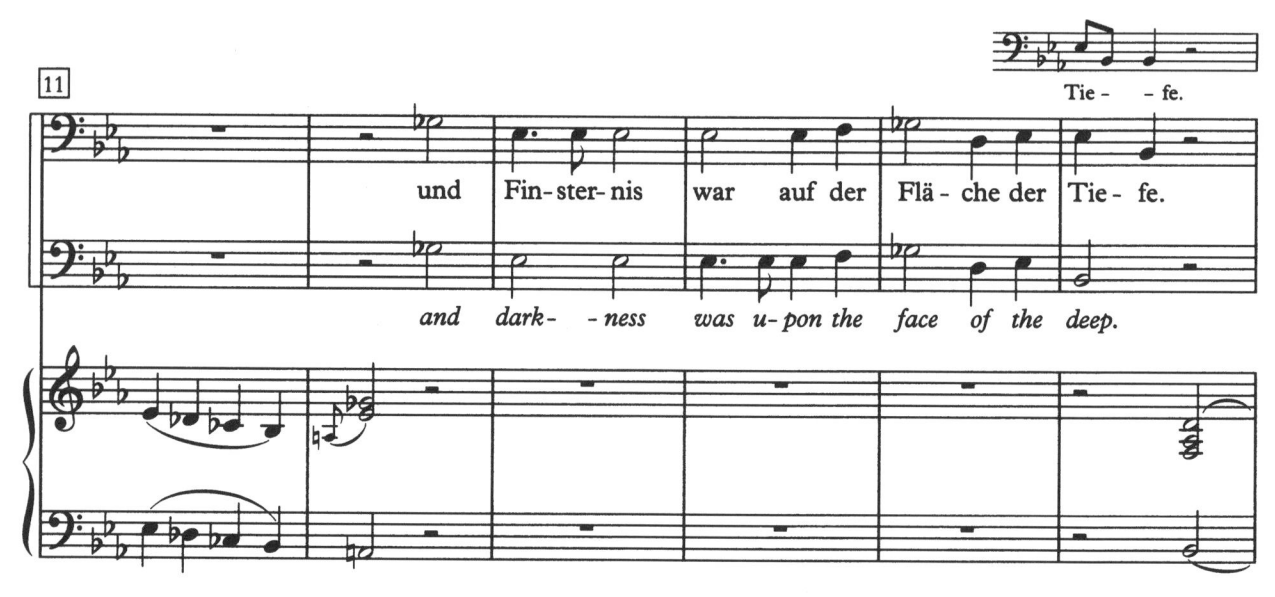

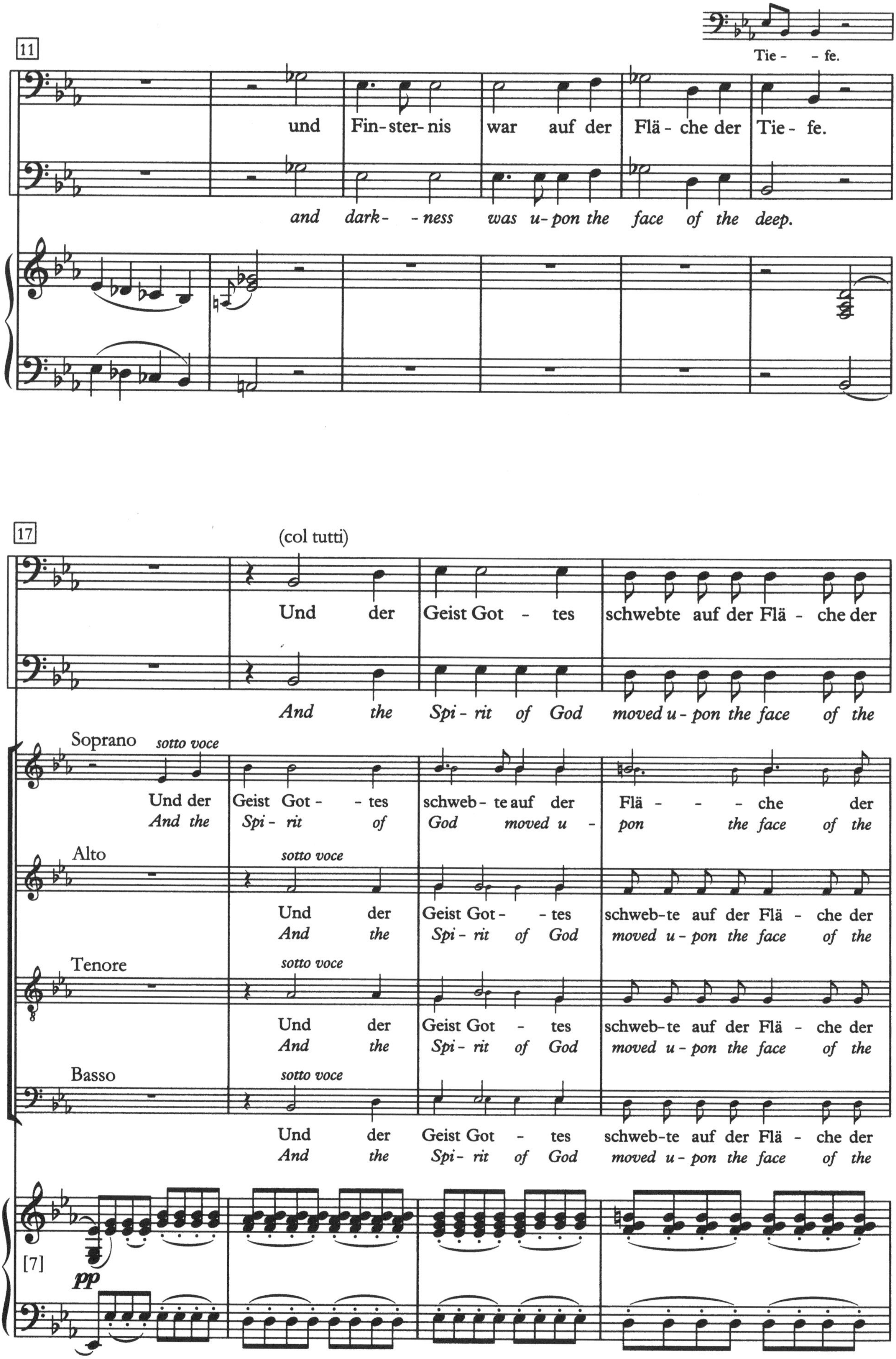
Tie- - fe.
11
und Fin-ster-nis war auf der Flä-che der Tie-fe.
and dark- -ness was u-pon the face of the deep.
17
(col tutti)
Und der Geist Got - tes schwebte auf der Flä - che der
And the Spi-rit of God moved u-pon the face of the
Soprano
sotto voce
Und der Geist Got- - tes schweb-te auf der Flä - - - che der
And the Spi- rit of God moved u - pon the face of the
Alto
sotto voce
Und der Geist Got- - tes schweb-te auf der Flä - che der
And the Spi-rit of God moved u-pon the face of the
Tenore
sotto voce
Und der Geist Got - tes schweb-te auf der Flä - che der
And the Spi-rit of God moved u-pon the face of the
Basso
sotto voce
Und der Geist Got - tes schweb-te auf der Flä - che der
And the Spi-rit of God moved u-pon the face of the
[7]
pp

Recitativo

Uriel: Und Gott sah das Licht, daß es gut war; und Gott schied das Licht von der Finsternis.

And God saw the Light, that it was good; and God divided the Light from the darkness.

attacca subito

Nr. 3 · No. 3
Arie und Chor · Aria and Chorus

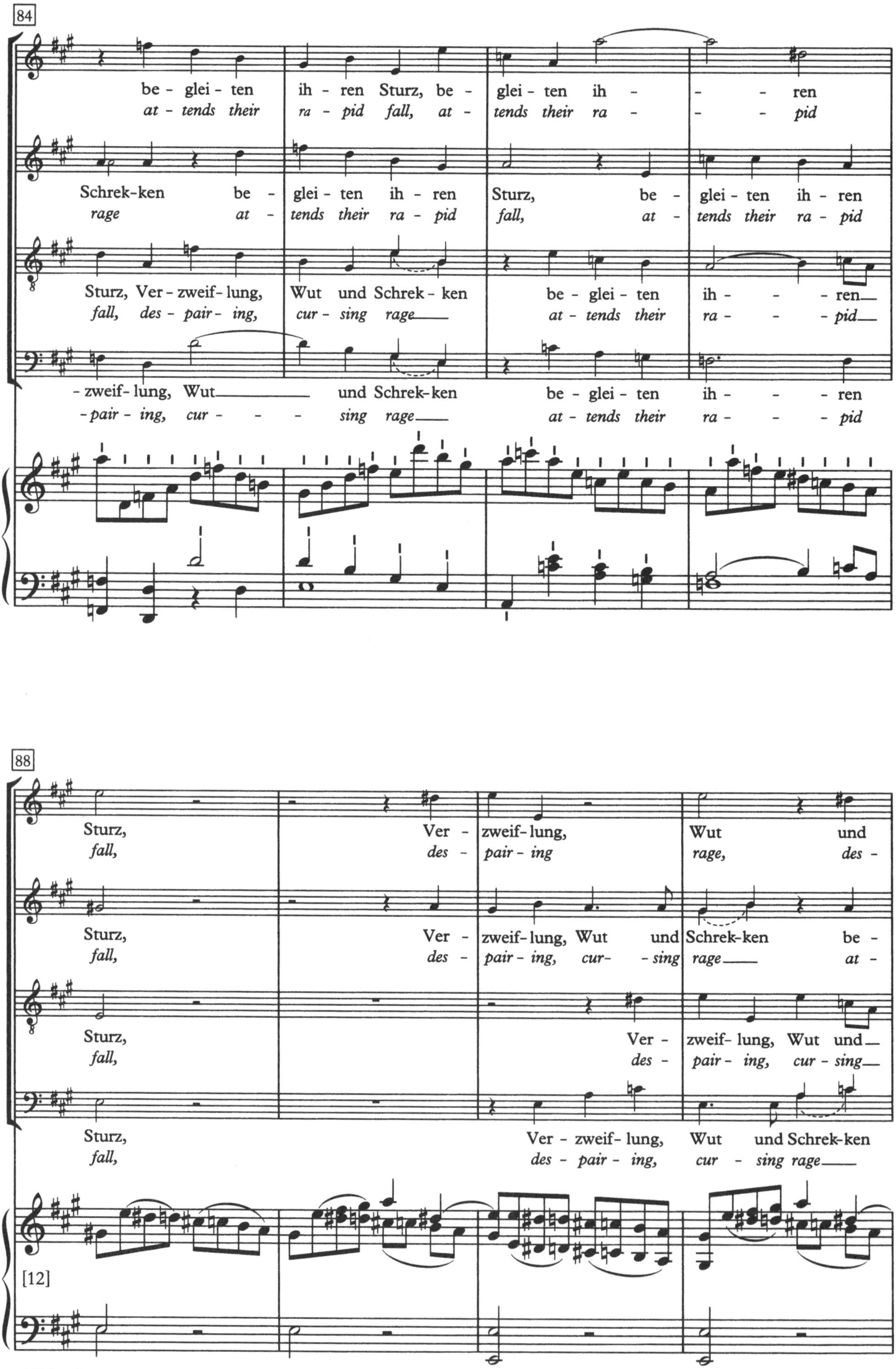
84
be - glei - ten ih - ren Sturz, be - glei - ten ih - - - ren
at - tends their ra - pid fall, at - tends their ra - - - pid
Schrek-ken be - glei - ten ih - ren Sturz, be - glei - ten ih - ren
rage at - tends their ra - pid fall, at - tends their ra - pid
Sturz, Ver - zweif - lung, Wut und Schrek - ken be - glei - ten ih - - - ren
fall, des - pair - ing, cur - sing rage at - tends their ra - - - pid
- zweif - lung, Wut und Schrek-ken be - glei - ten ih - - - ren
- pair - ing, cur - - - sing rage at - tends their ra - - - pid
88
Sturz, Ver - zweif - lung, Wut und
fall, des - pair - ing rage, des -
Sturz, Ver - zweif - lung, Wut und Schrek-ken be -
fall, des - pair - ing, cur- - sing rage at -
Sturz, Ver - zweif - lung, Wut und
fall, des - pair - ing, cur - sing
Sturz, Ver - zweif - lung, Wut und Schrek-ken
fall, des - pair - ing, cur - sing rage
[12]

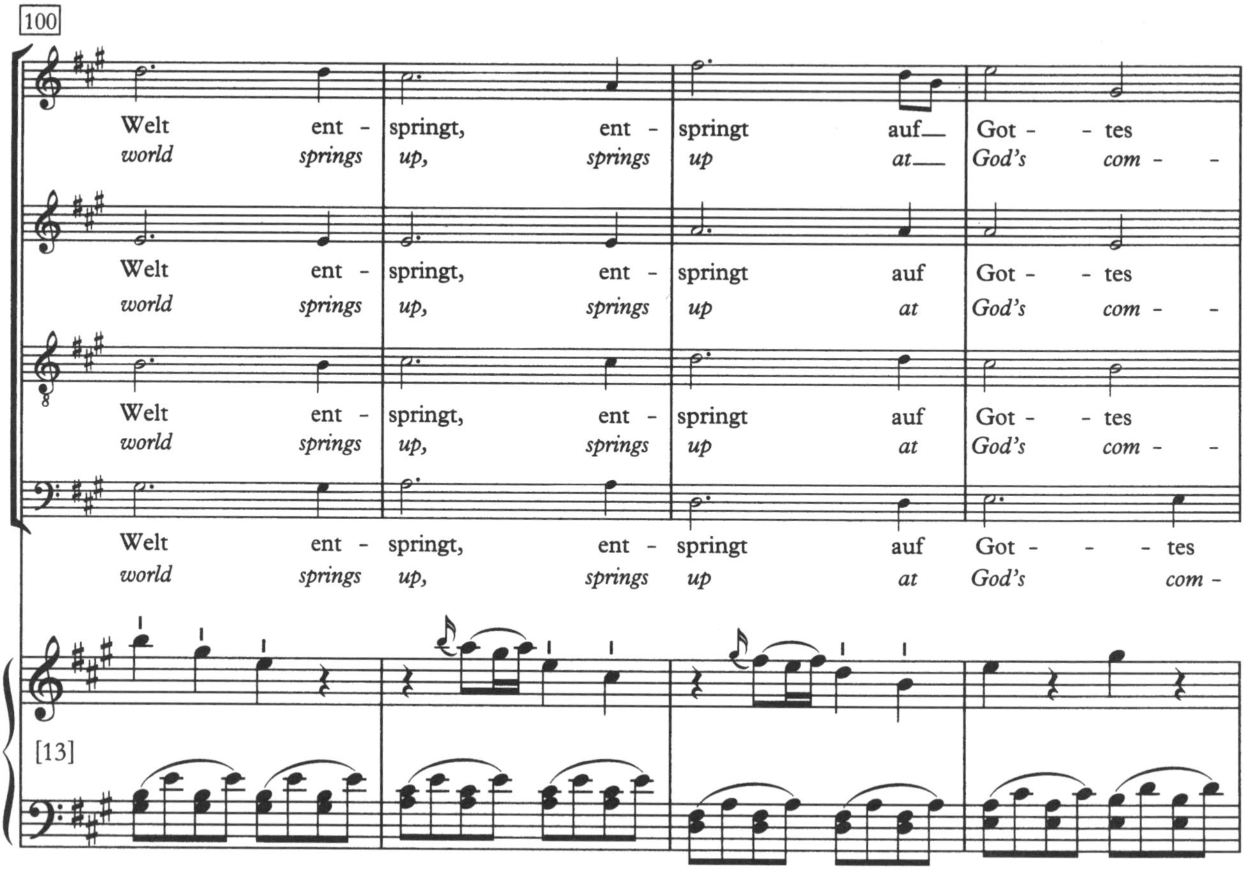
100
Welt ent - springt, ent - springt auf Got - - tes
world springs up, springs up at God's com - -
Welt ent - springt, ent - springt auf Got - - tes
world springs up, springs up at God's com - -
Welt ent - springt, ent - springt auf Got - - tes
world springs up, springs up at God's com - -
Welt ent - springt, ent - springt auf Got - - - tes
world springs up, springs up at God's com -
[13]

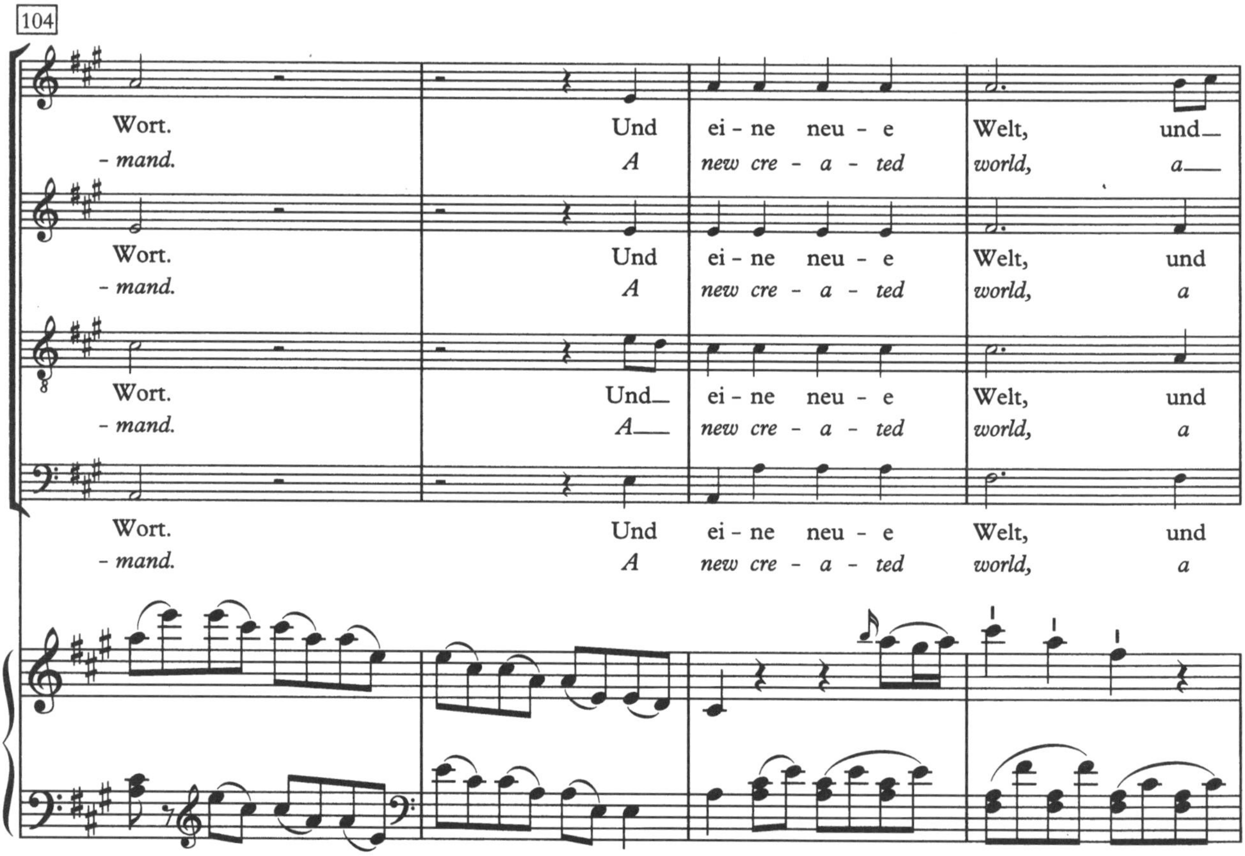
104
Wort. Und ei - ne neu - e Welt, und
- mand. A new cre - a - ted world, a
Wort. Und ei - ne neu - e Welt, und
- mand. A new cre - a - ted world, a
Wort. Und ei - ne neu - e Welt, und
- mand. A new cre - a - ted world, a
Wort. Und ei - ne neu - e Welt, und
- mand. A new cre - a - ted world, a

17

128

eine neue Welt, und eine neue Welt ent-
new created world, a new created world springs

eine neue Welt, und eine neue Welt ent-
new created world, a new created world springs

eine neue Welt, und eine neue Welt ent-
new created world, a new created world springs

eine neue Welt, und eine neue Welt ent-
new created world, a new created world springs

+ Fl.

[15] Archi

132

-springt, entspringt auf Gottes Wort.
up, springs up at God's command.

-springt, entspringt auf Gottes Wort.
up, springs up at God's command.

-springt, entspringt auf Gottes Wort.
up, springs up at God's command.

-springt, entspringt auf Gottes Wort.
up, springs up at God's command.

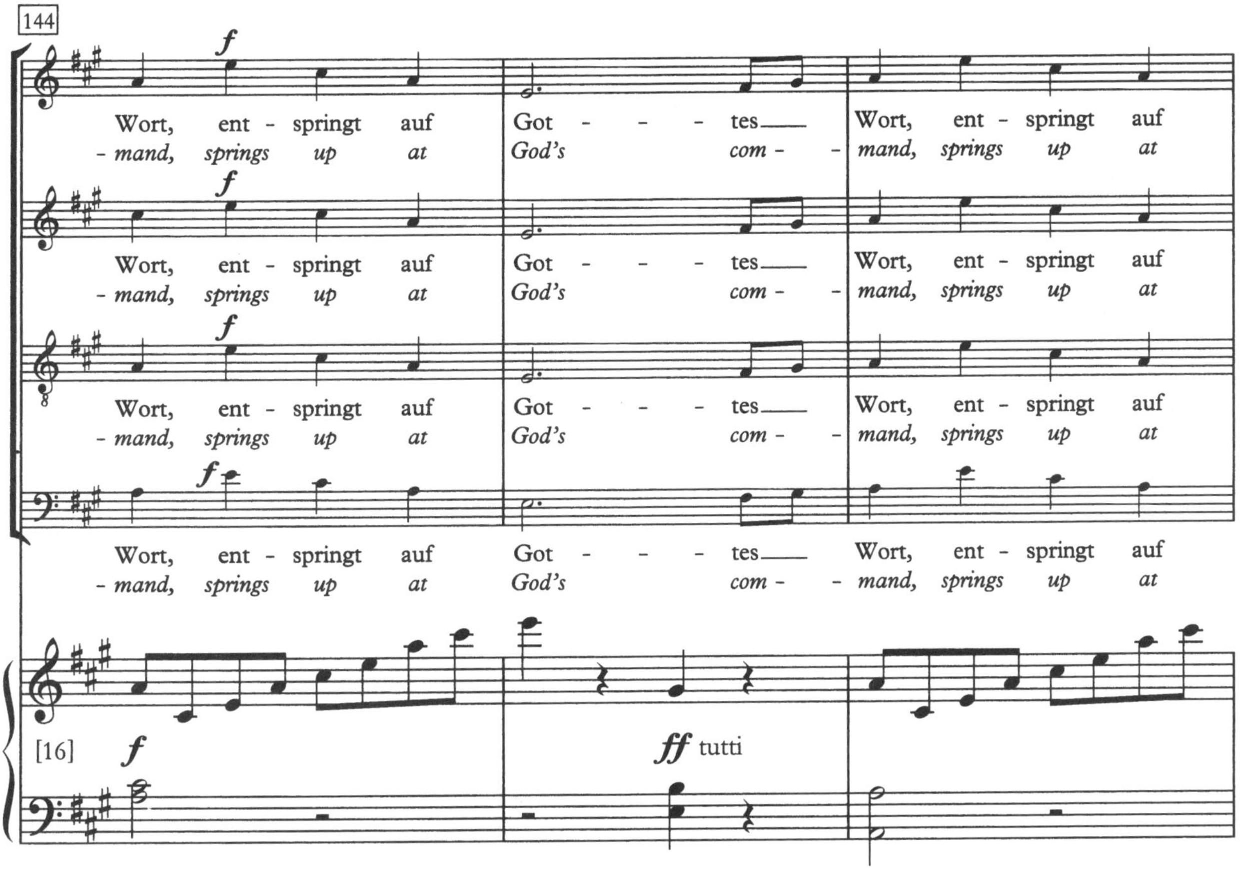
144
f
Wort, ent - springt auf Got - - - tes Wort, ent - springt auf
- mand, springs up at God's com - - mand, springs up at
[16]
ff tutti

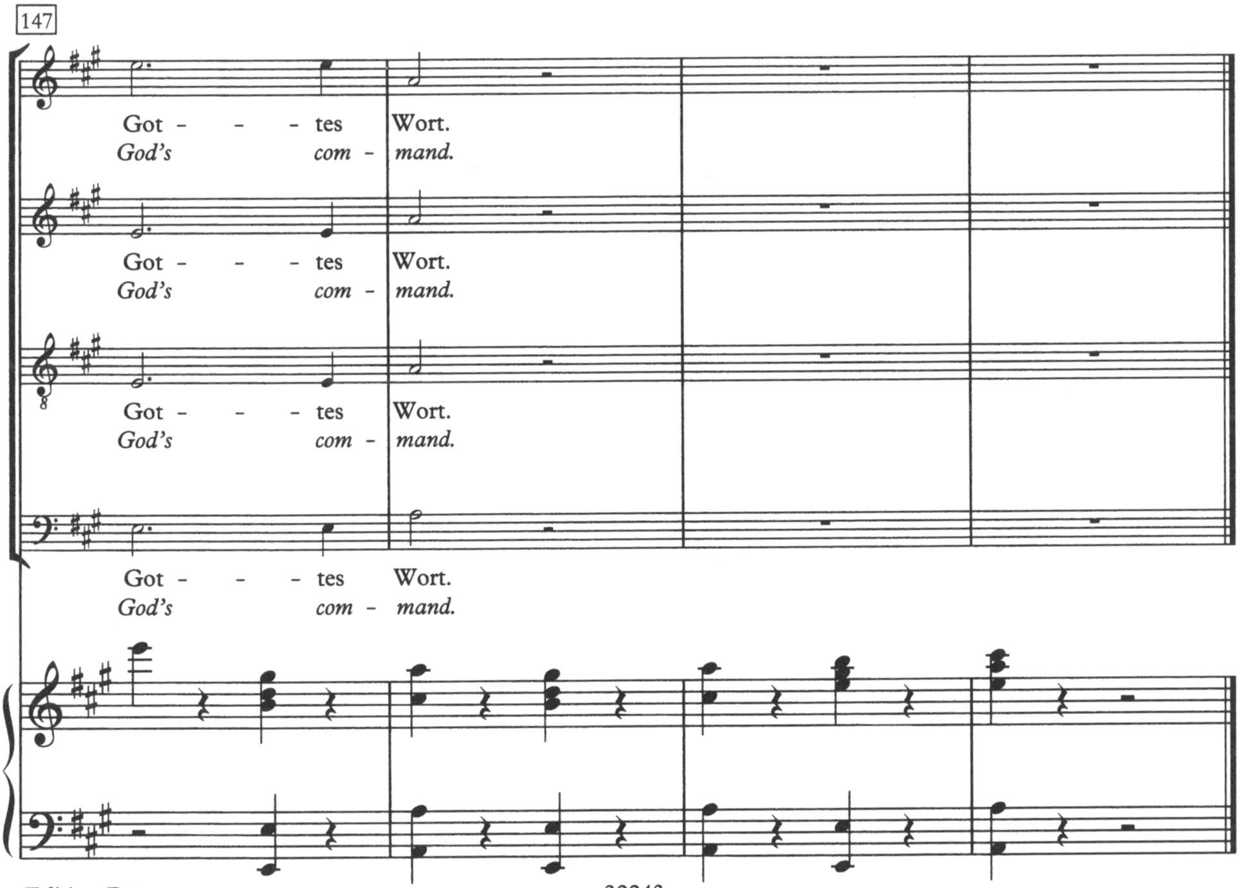
147
Got - - - tes Wort.
God's com - mand.

Nr. 4 · No. 4
Rezitativ (Raphael) · Recitative (Raphael)

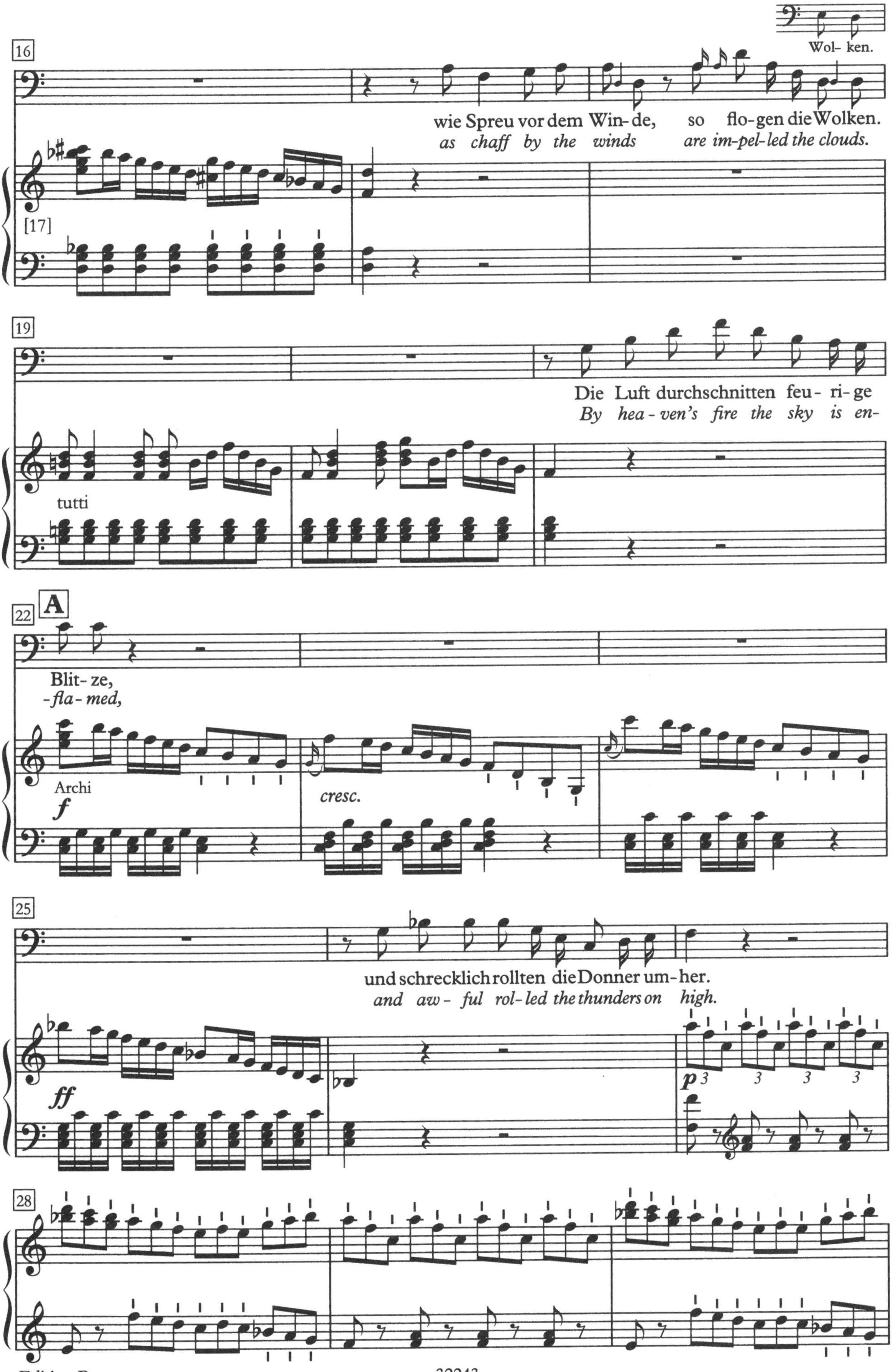
Wol- ken.
16
wie Spreu vor dem Win- de, so flo- gen die Wolken.
as chaff by the winds are im-pel-led the clouds.
[17]
19
Die Luft durchschnitten feu- ri- ge
By hea- ven's fire the sky is en-
tutti
A
22
Blit- ze,
-fla- med,
Archi
f
cresc.
25
und schrecklich rollten die Donner um- her.
and aw- ful rol- led the thunders on high.
ff
p
28

Nr. 7 · No. 7
Arie · Aria

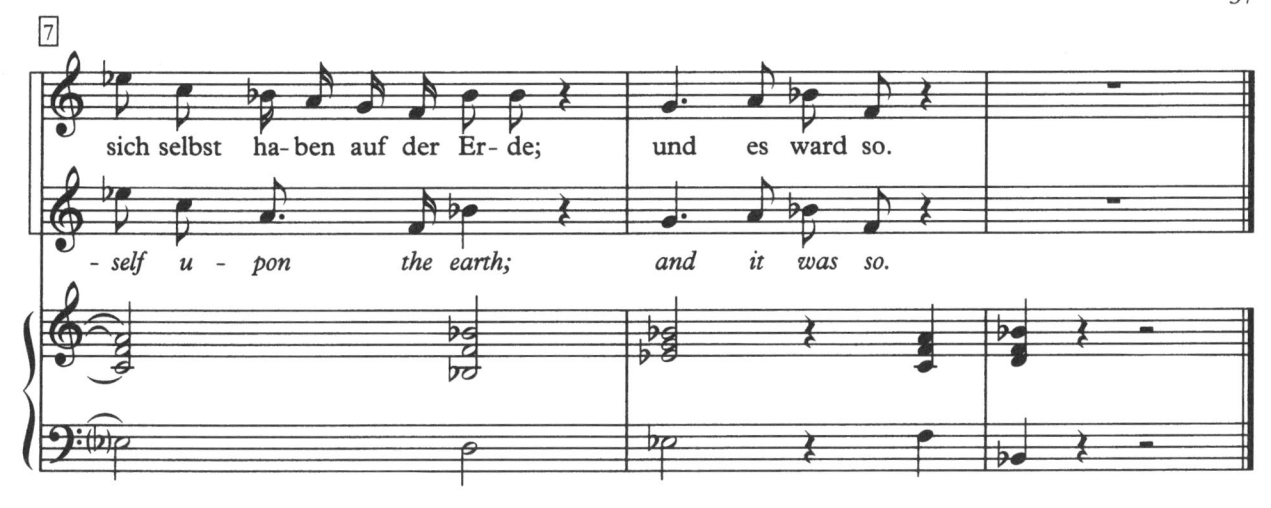

Nr. 11 · No. 11
Chor · Chorus

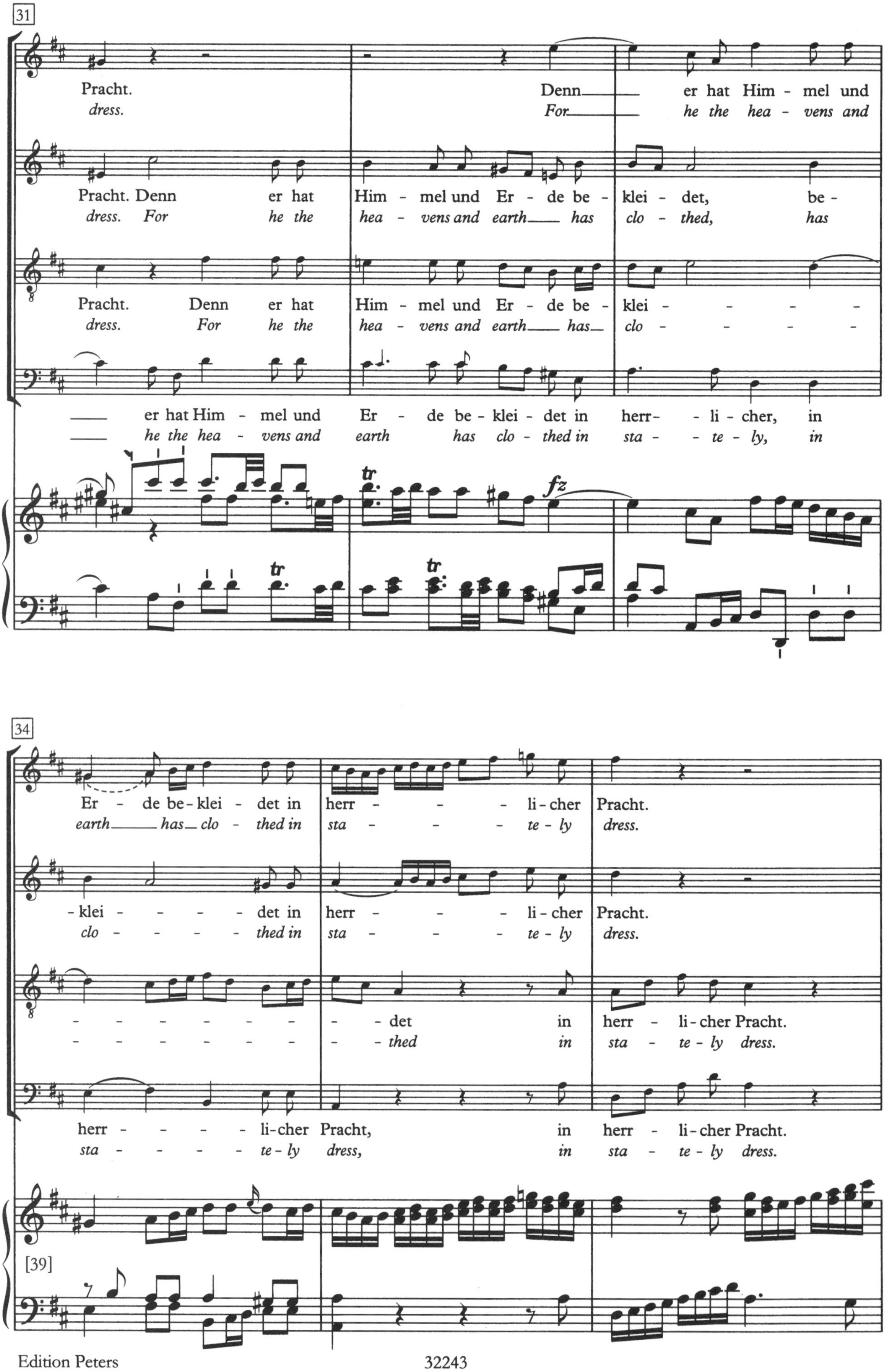
31
Pracht. Denn er hat Him - mel und
dress. For he the hea - vens and
Pracht. Denn er hat Him - mel und Er - de be - klei - det, be -
dress. For he the hea - vens and earth has clo - thed, has
Pracht. Denn er hat Him - mel und Er - de be - klei -
dress. For he the hea - vens and earth has clo -
er hat Him - mel und Er - de be - klei - det in herr - li - cher, in
he the hea - vens and earth has clo - thed in sta - te - ly, in
tr
fz
34
Er - de be - klei - det in herr - li - cher Pracht.
earth has clo - thed in sta - te - ly dress.
- klei - det in herr - li - cher Pracht.
clo - thed in sta - te - ly dress.
- det in herr - li - cher Pracht.
- thed in sta - te - ly dress.
herr - li - cher Pracht, in herr - li - cher Pracht.
sta - te - ly dress, in sta - te - ly dress.
[39]

Nr. 12 · No. 12
Rezitativ · Recitative

Nr. 13 · No. 13
Rezitativ · Recitative

Nr. 14 · No. 14
Chor mit Soli · Chorus with Soli

Allegro

Soprano: Die Him-mel er-zäh-len die Eh-re Got-tes;
The hea-vens are tell-ing the glo-ry of God;

Alto: Die Him-mel er-zäh-len die Eh-re Got-tes;
The hea-vens are tell-ing the glo-ry of God;

Tenore: Die Him-mel er-zäh-len die Eh-re Got-tes;
The hea-vens are tell-ing the glo-ry of God;

Basso: Die Him-mel er-zäh-len die Eh-re Got-tes;
The hea-vens are tell-ing the glo-ry of God;

[44] *f* tutti   Archi

und sei-ner Hän-de Werk zeigt
the won-der of his works dis-

und sei-ner Hän-de Werk zeigt
the won-der of his works dis-

und sei-ner Hän-de Werk zeigt
the won-der of his works dis-

und sei-ner Hän-de Werk zeigt
the won-der of his works dis-

tutti   *fz*

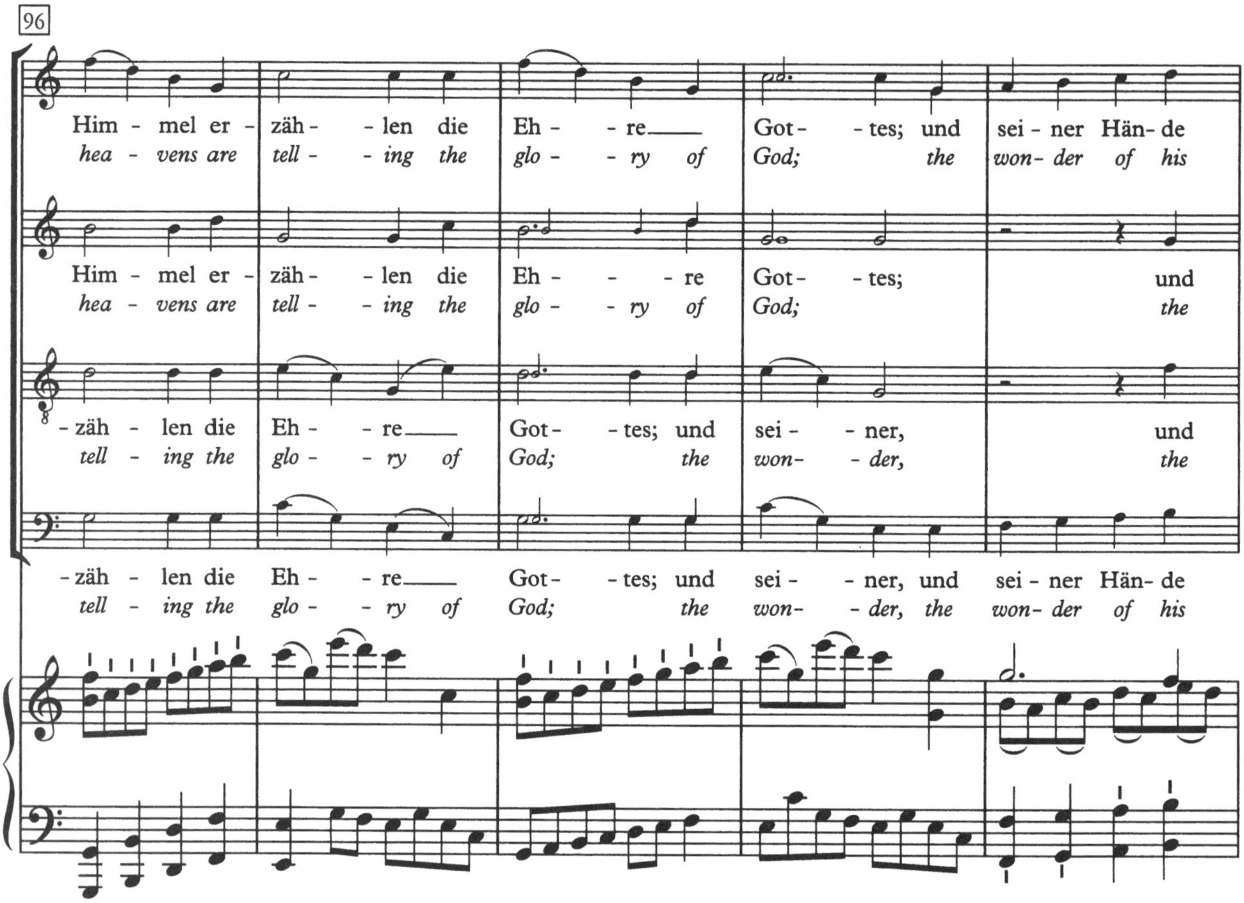
96
Him - mel er - zäh - - len die Eh - - re Got - - tes; und sei - ner Hän - de
hea - vens are tell - - ing the glo - - ry of God; the won - der of his
Him - mel er - zäh - - len die Eh - - - re Got - - tes; und
hea - vens are tell - - ing the glo - - ry of God; the
- zäh - len die Eh - - re Got - - tes; und sei - - ner, und
tell - ing the glo - - ry of God; the won - - der, the
- zäh - len die Eh - - re Got - - tes; und sei - - ner, und sei - ner Hän - de
tell - ing the glo - - ry of God; the won - - der, the won - der of his

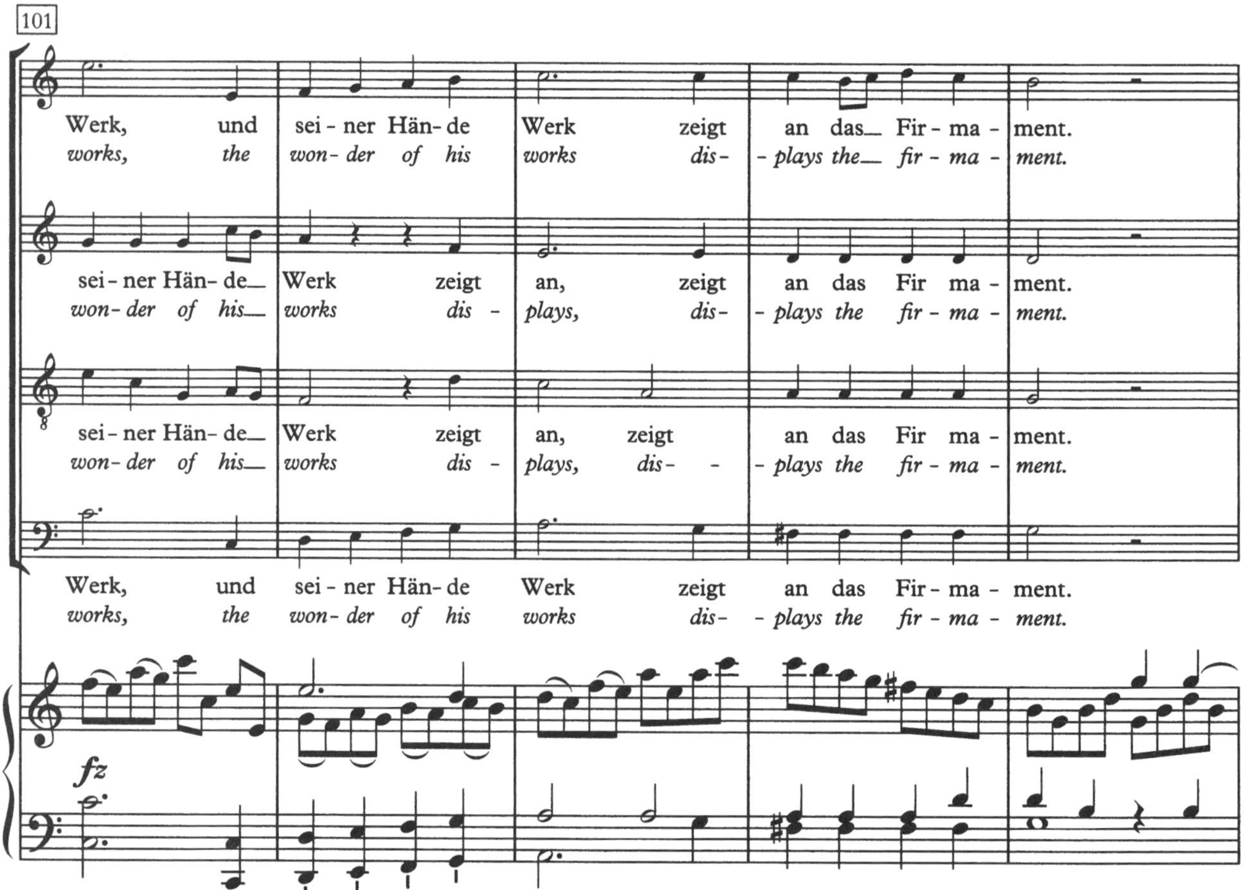
101
Werk, und sei - ner Hän - de Werk zeigt an das Fir - ma - ment.
works, the won - der of his works dis - - plays the fir - ma - ment.
sei - ner Hän - de Werk zeigt an, zeigt an das Fir ma - ment.
won - der of his works dis - plays, dis - - plays the fir - ma - ment.
sei - ner Hän - de Werk zeigt an, zeigt an das Fir ma - ment.
won - der of his works dis - plays, dis - - plays the fir - ma - ment.
Werk, und sei - ner Hän - de Werk zeigt an das Fir - ma - ment.
works, the won - der of his works dis - - plays the fir - ma - ment.
fz

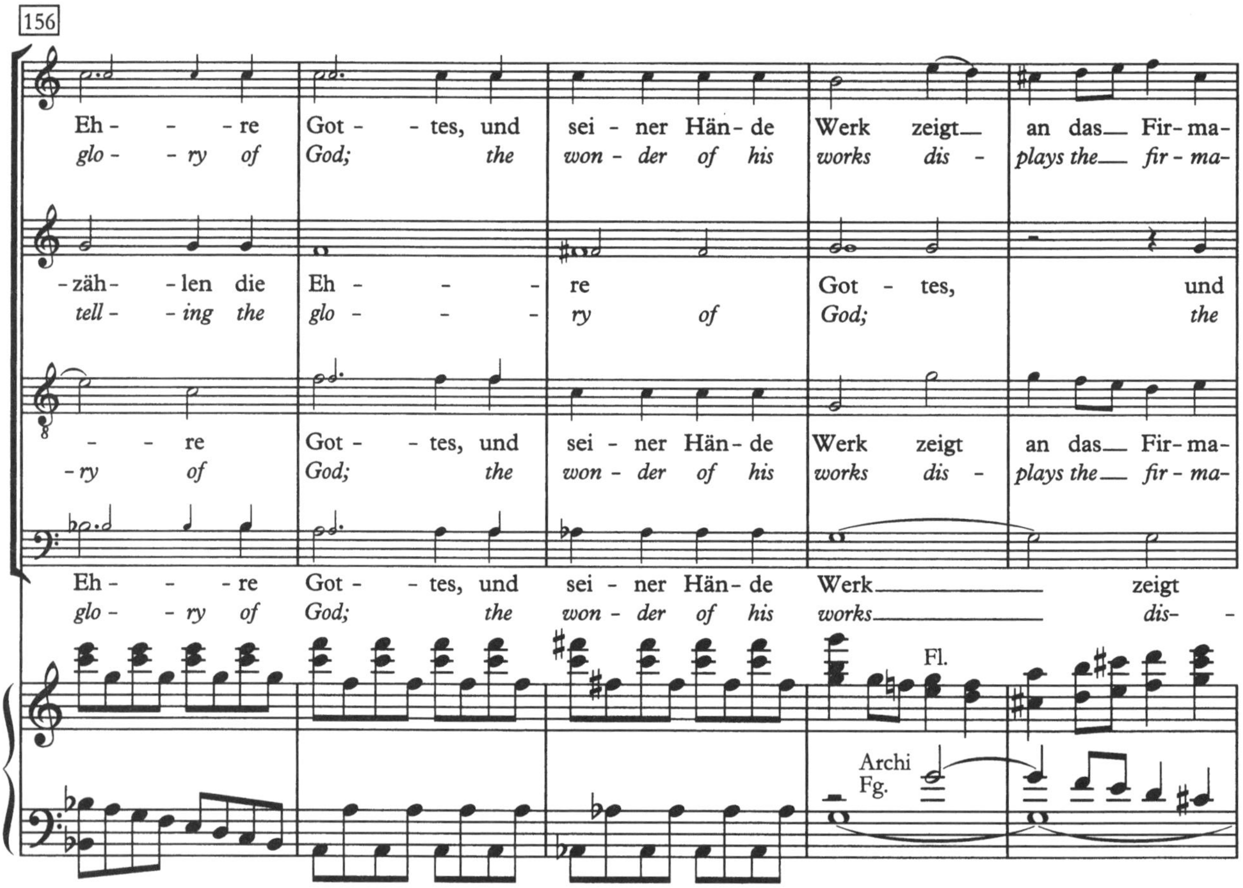
156
Eh - - re Got - - tes, und sei - ner Hän - de Werk zeigt an das Fir - ma-
glo - - ry of God; the won - der of his works dis - plays the fir - ma-
-zäh - - len die Eh - - - re Got - tes, und
tell - - ing the glo - - - ry of God; the
- - re Got - - tes, und sei - ner Hän - de Werk zeigt an das Fir - ma-
-ry of God; the won - der of his works dis - plays the fir - ma-
Eh - - re Got - - tes, und sei - ner Hän - de Werk zeigt
glo - - ry of God; the won - der of his works dis-
Fl.
Archi
Fg.

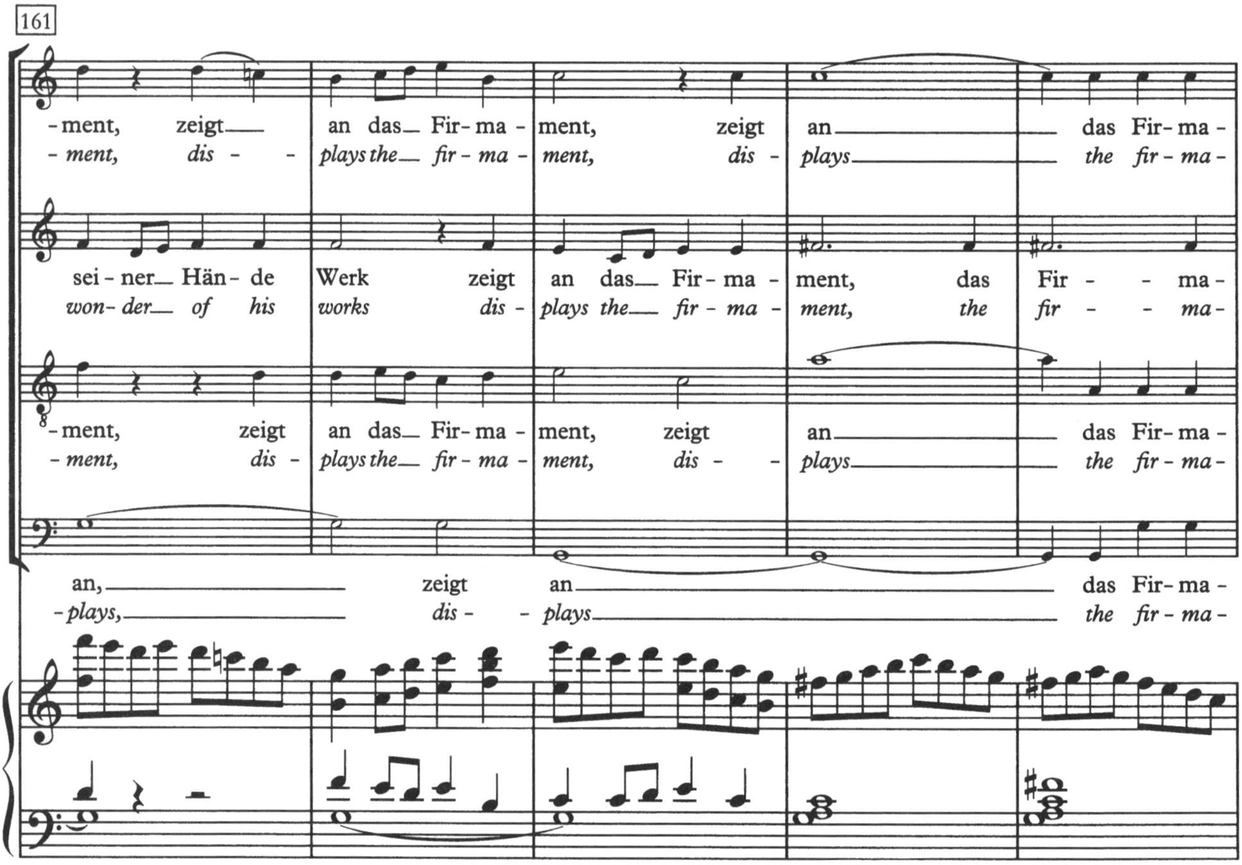
161
-ment, zeigt an das Fir - ma - ment, zeigt an das Fir - ma -
-ment, dis - plays the fir - ma - ment, dis - plays the fir - ma -
sei - ner Hän - de Werk zeigt an das Fir - ma - ment, das Fir - - ma-
won - der of his works dis - plays the fir - ma - ment, the fir - - ma-
-ment, zeigt an das Fir - ma - ment, zeigt an das Fir - ma -
-ment, dis - plays the fir - ma - ment, dis - plays the fir - ma -
an, zeigt an das Fir - ma -
-plays, dis - plays the fir - ma -

Teil II · Part II
Nr. 15 · No. 15
Rezitativ · Recitative

Nr. 16 · No. 16
Arie · Aria

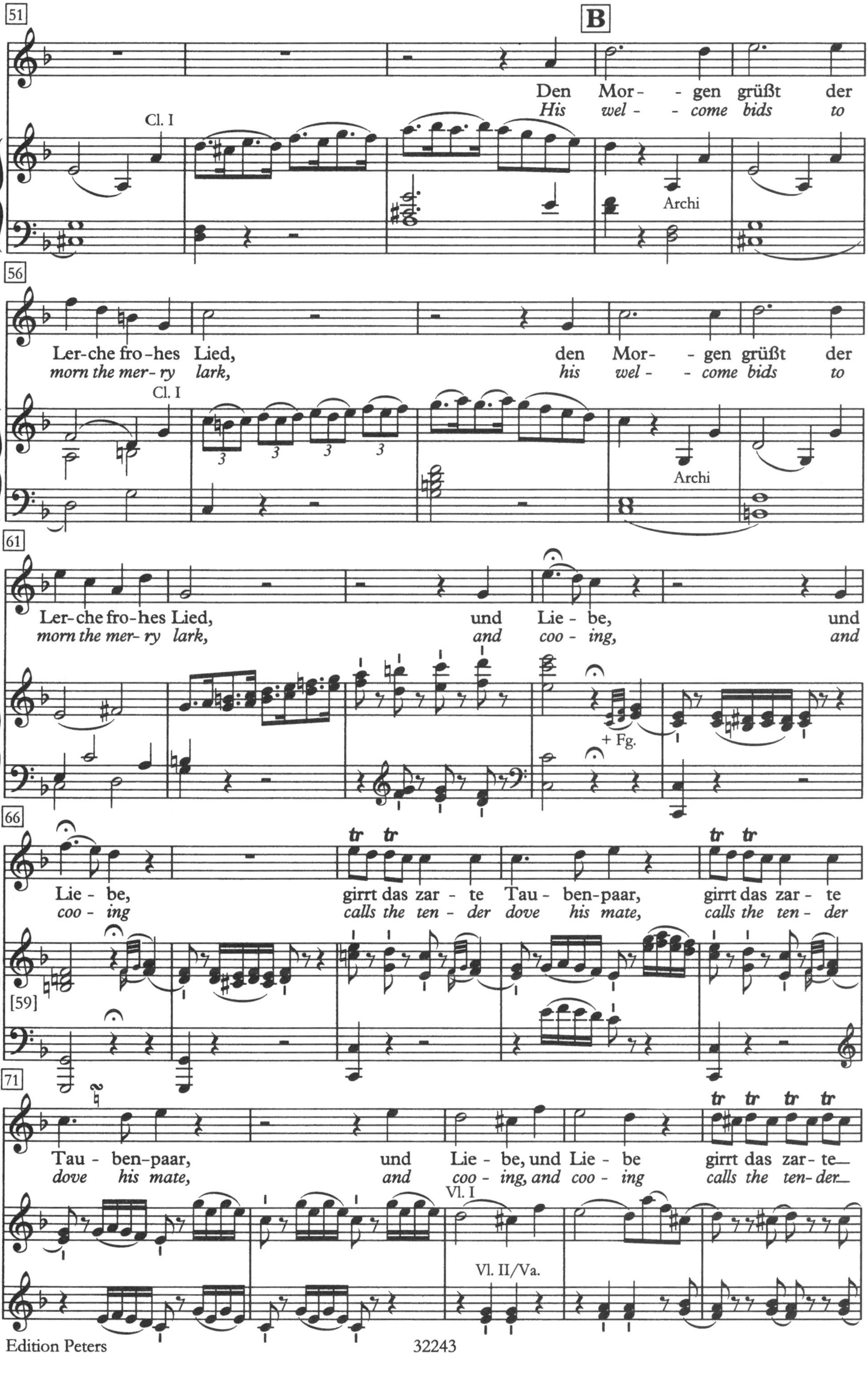
51
B
Den Mor - - gen grüßt der
His wel - - come bids to
Cl. I
Archi
56
Ler-che fro-hes Lied,
morn the mer-ry lark,
den Mor - - gen grüßt der
his wel - - come bids to
Cl. I
Archi
61
Ler-che fro-hes Lied,
morn the mer-ry lark,
und Lie - be,
and coo - ing,
und
and
+ Fg.
66
Lie - be,
coo - ing
girrt das zar - te Tau - ben-paar, girrt das zar - te
calls the ten - der dove his mate, calls the ten - der
tr tr
[59]
71
Tau - ben-paar,
dove his mate,
und Lie - be, und Lie - be
and coo - ing, and coo - ing
girrt das zar - te
calls the ten - der
Vl. I
Vl. II/Va.

Nr. 17 · No. 7
Rezitativ · Recitative

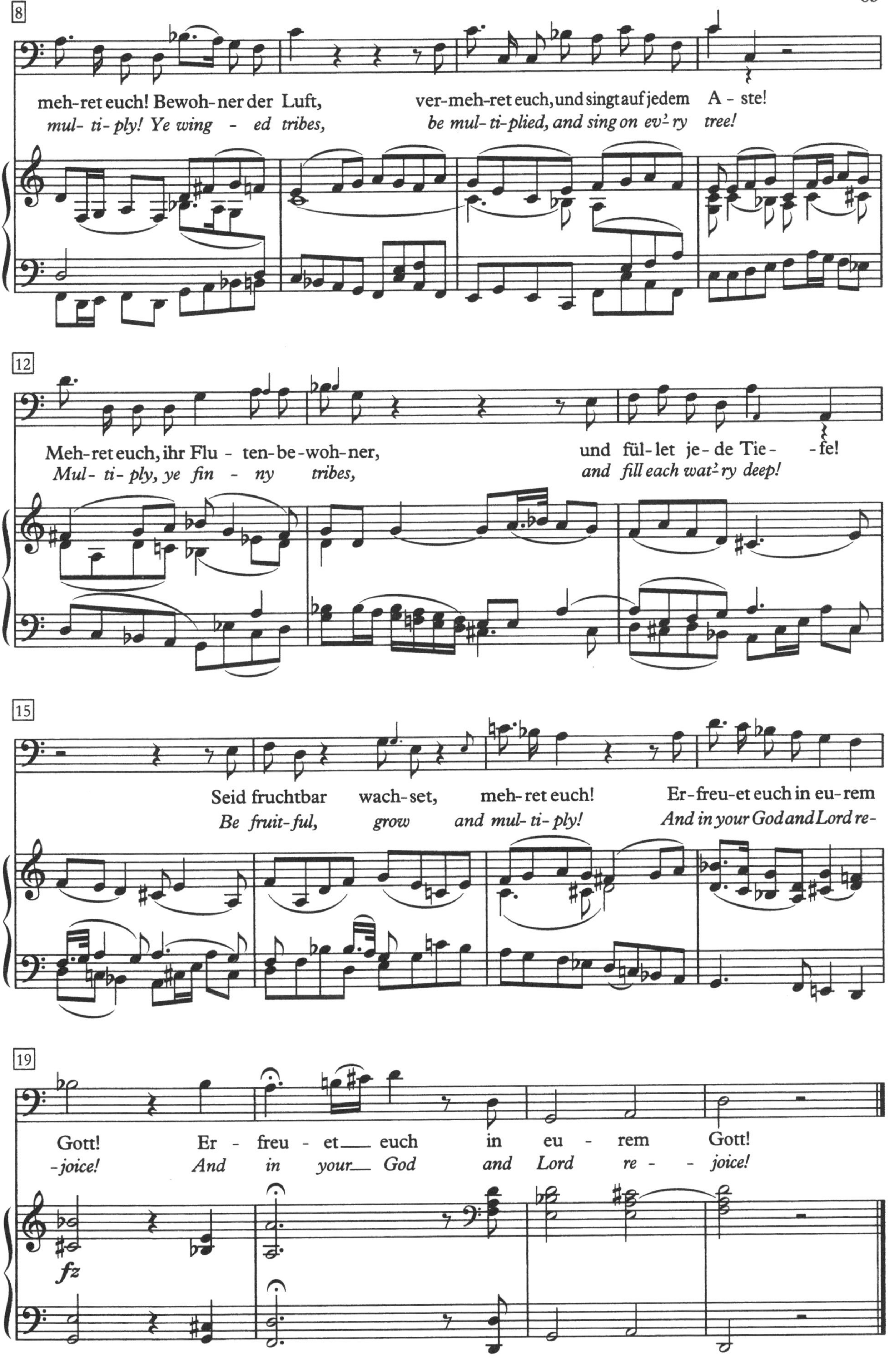
8
meh-ret euch! Bewoh-ner der Luft, ver-meh-ret euch, und singt auf jedem A - ste!
mul- ti- ply! Ye wing - ed tribes, be mul- ti-plied, and sing on ev'- ry tree!
12
Meh-ret euch, ihr Flu - ten-be-woh-ner, und fül-let je-de Tie- -fe!
Mul- ti- ply, ye fin - ny tribes, and fill each wat'- ry deep!
15
Seid fruchtbar wach-set, meh-ret euch! Er-freu-et euch in eu-rem
Be fruit-ful, grow and mul- ti- ply! And in your God and Lord re-
19
Gott! Er - freu - et euch in eu - rem Gott!
-joice! And in your God and Lord re - - joice!
fz

Nr. 20 · No. 20
Terzett und Chor · Trio and Chorus

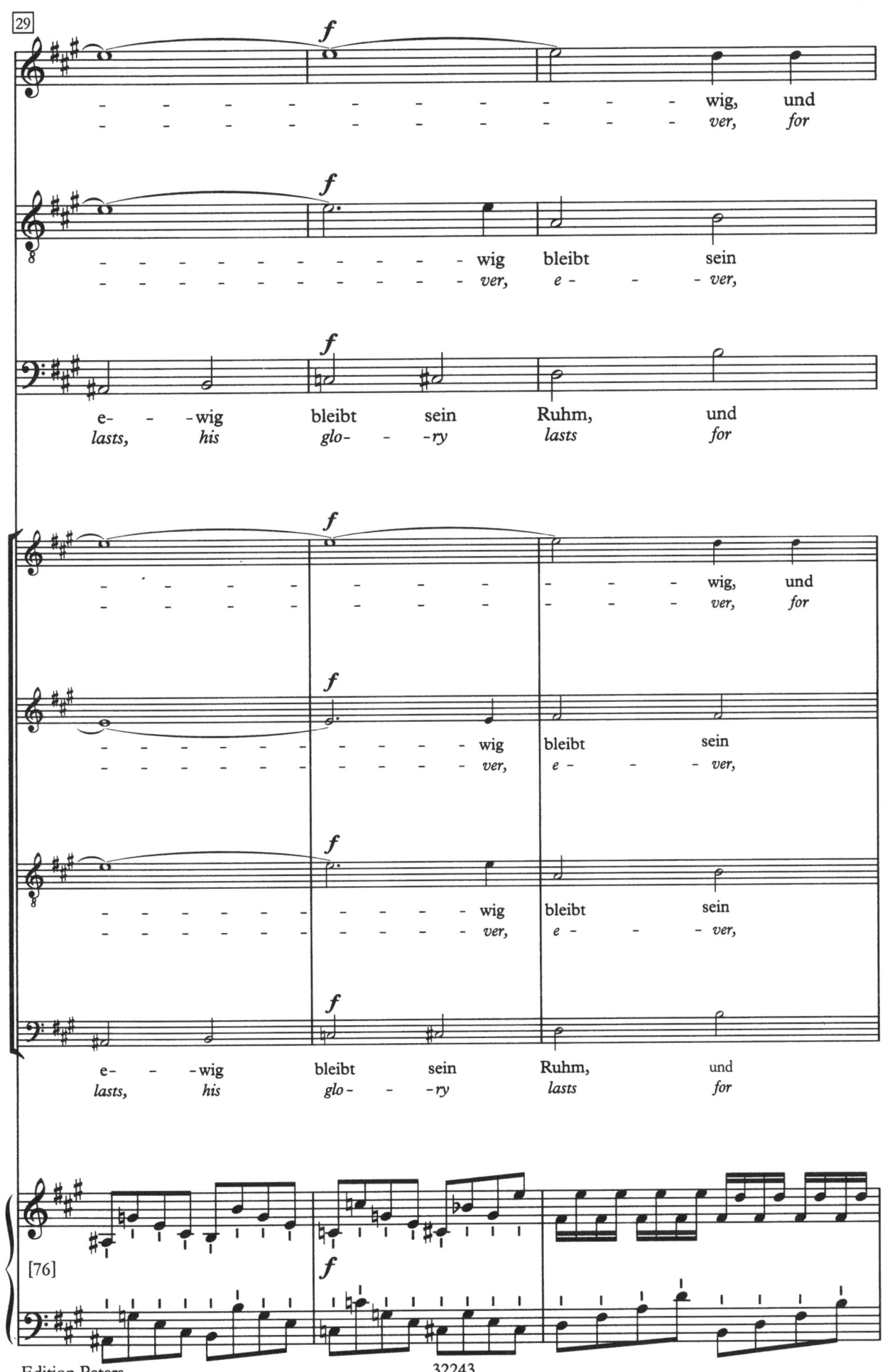

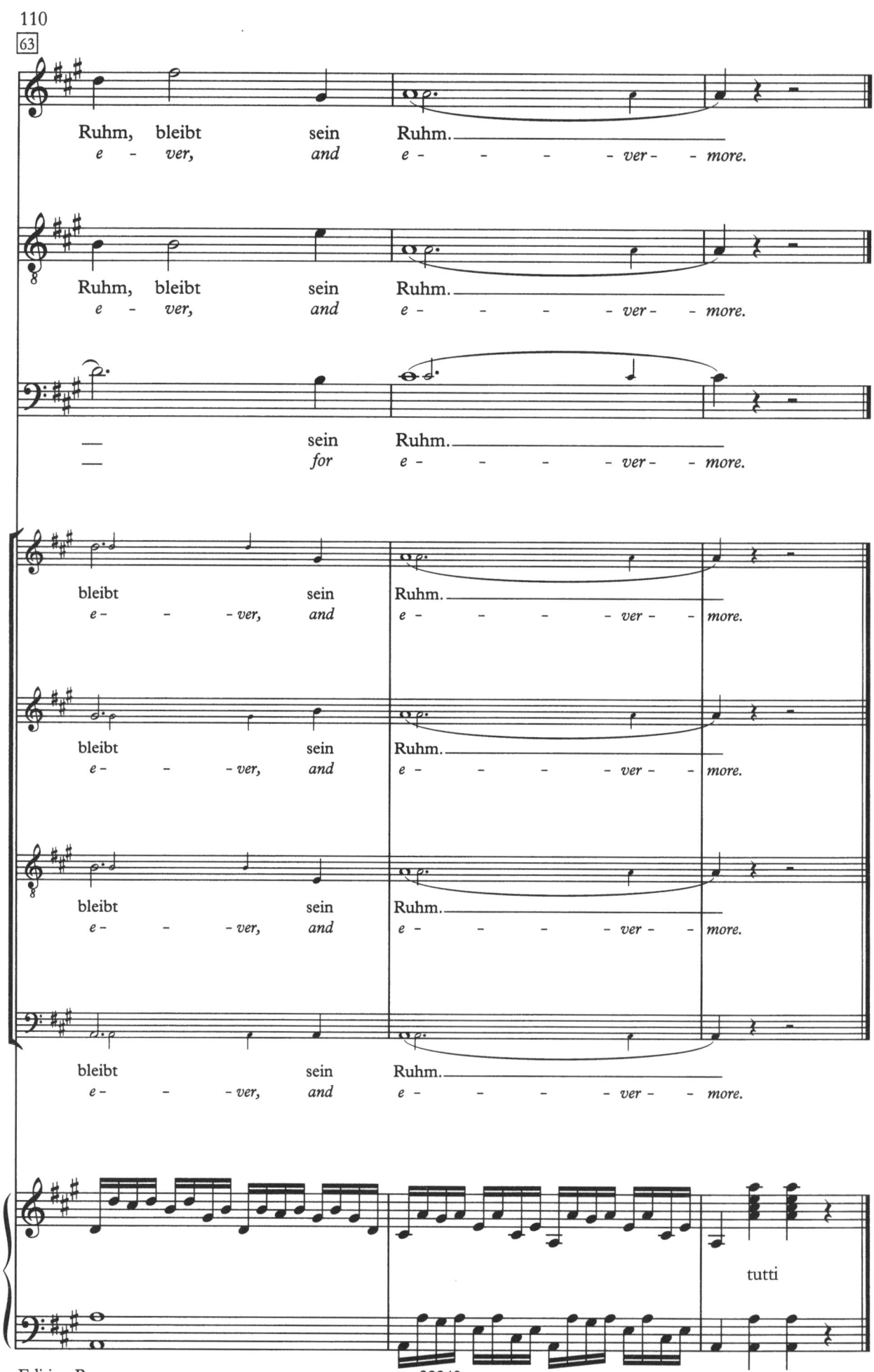

nun prangt in ih-rem Schmuk-ke die Er-de.
earth smiles in all her rich at-tire.

Die Luft er-füllt das leich-te Ge-fie-der;
The room of air with fowl is fill'd;

die Was-ser schwellt der Fi-sche Ge-wim-mel;
the wa-ter swell'd by shoals of fish;

den Bo-den drückt der Tie-re
by hea-vy beasts the ground is

Nr. 24 · No. 24
Rezitativ · Recitative

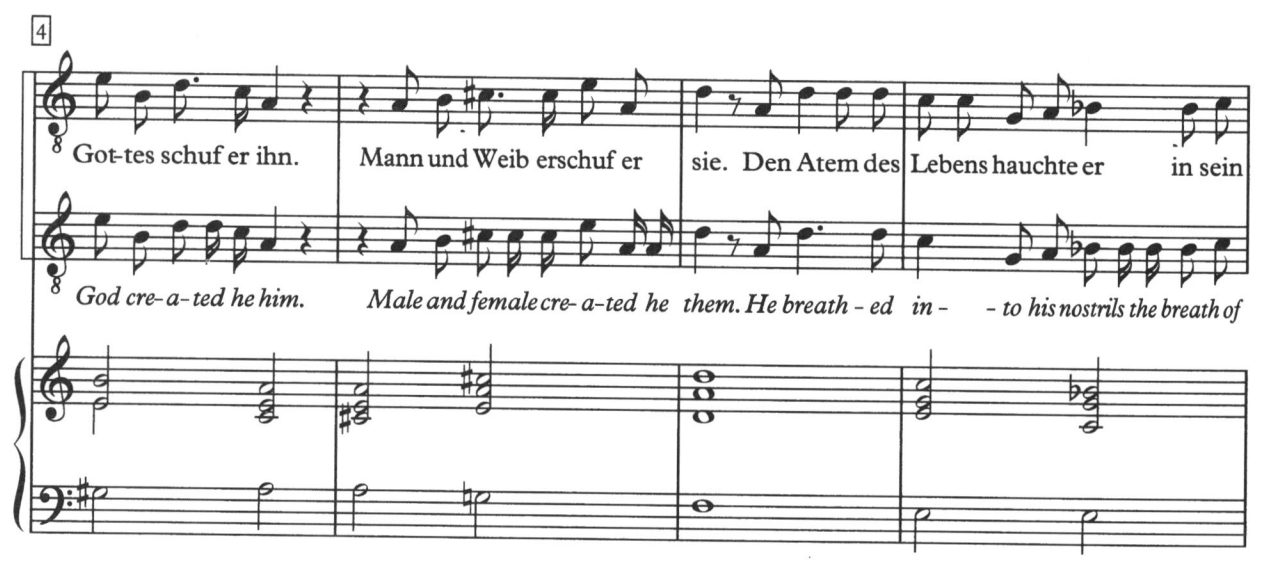

Nr. 25 · No. 25
Arie · Aria

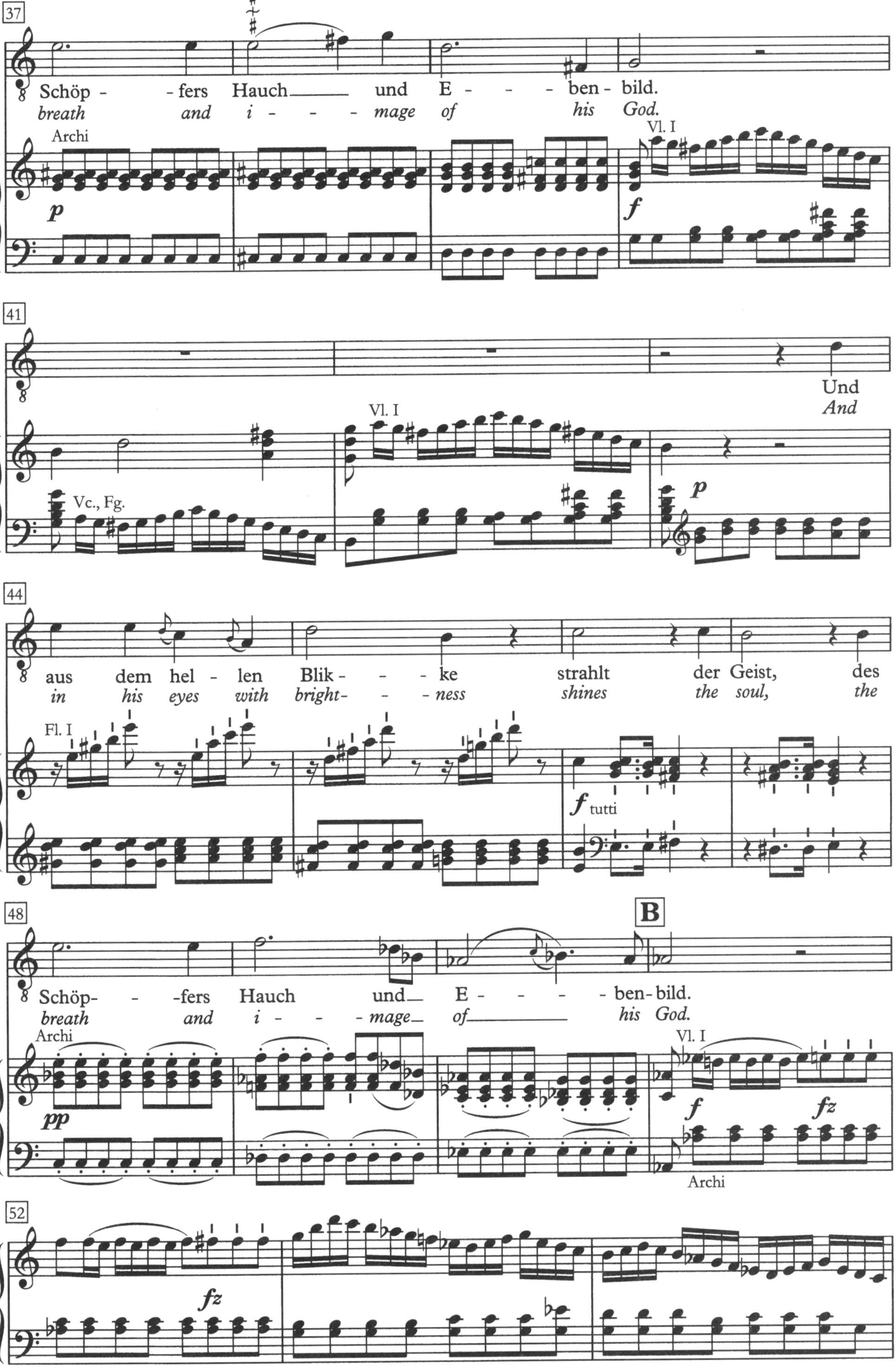
37
Schöp - -fers Hauch und E - - - ben - bild.
breath and i - - - mage of his God.
Archi
p
Vl. I
f
41
Vc., Fg.
Vl. I
p
Und
And
44
aus dem hel - len Blik - - - ke strahlt der Geist, des
in his eyes with bright- - - ness shines the soul, the
Fl. I
f tutti
48
B
Schöp- - -fers Hauch und E - - - - ben - bild.
breath and i - - - mage of his God.
Archi
pp
Vl. I
f
fz
Archi
52
fz

Nr. 26 · No. 26
Rezitativ · Recitative

Nr. 27 · No. 27
Chor · Chorus

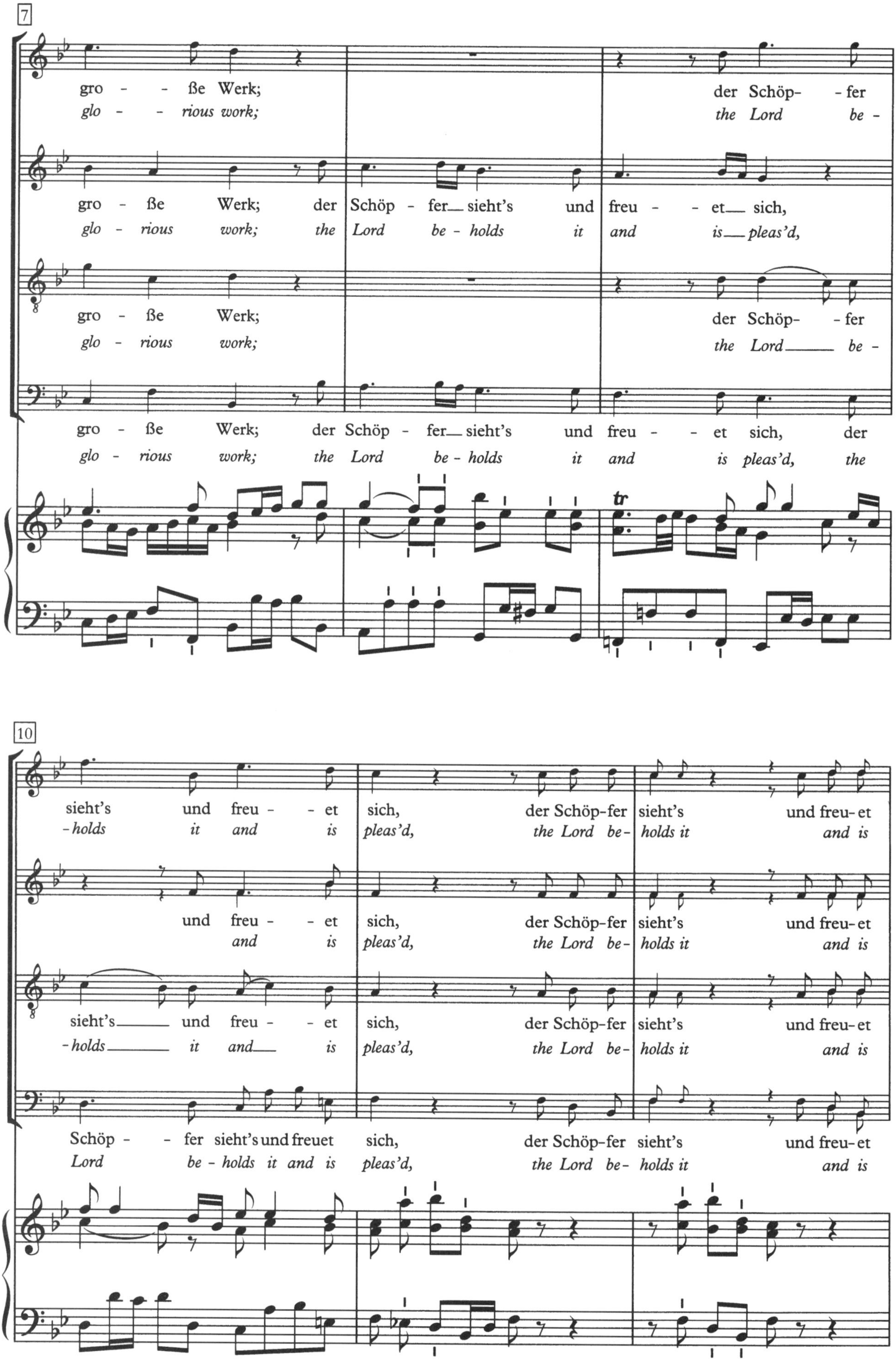
7
gro - ße Werk; der Schöp- fer
glo - rious work; the Lord be -
gro - ße Werk; der Schöp - fer sieht's und freu - et sich,
glo - rious work; the Lord be - holds it and is pleas'd,
gro - ße Werk; der Schöp- fer
glo - rious work; the Lord be -
gro - ße Werk; der Schöp - fer sieht's und freu - et sich, der
glo - rious work; the Lord be - holds it and is pleas'd, the
10
sieht's und freu - et sich, der Schöp-fer sieht's und freu-et
- holds it and is pleas'd, the Lord be- holds it and is
und freu - et sich, der Schöp-fer sieht's und freu-et
and is pleas'd, the Lord be- holds it and is
sieht's und freu - et sich, der Schöp-fer sieht's und freu-et
- holds it and is pleas'd, the Lord be- holds it and is
Schöp - fer sieht's und freuet sich, der Schöp-fer sieht's und freu-et
Lord be - holds it and is pleas'd, the Lord be- holds it and is

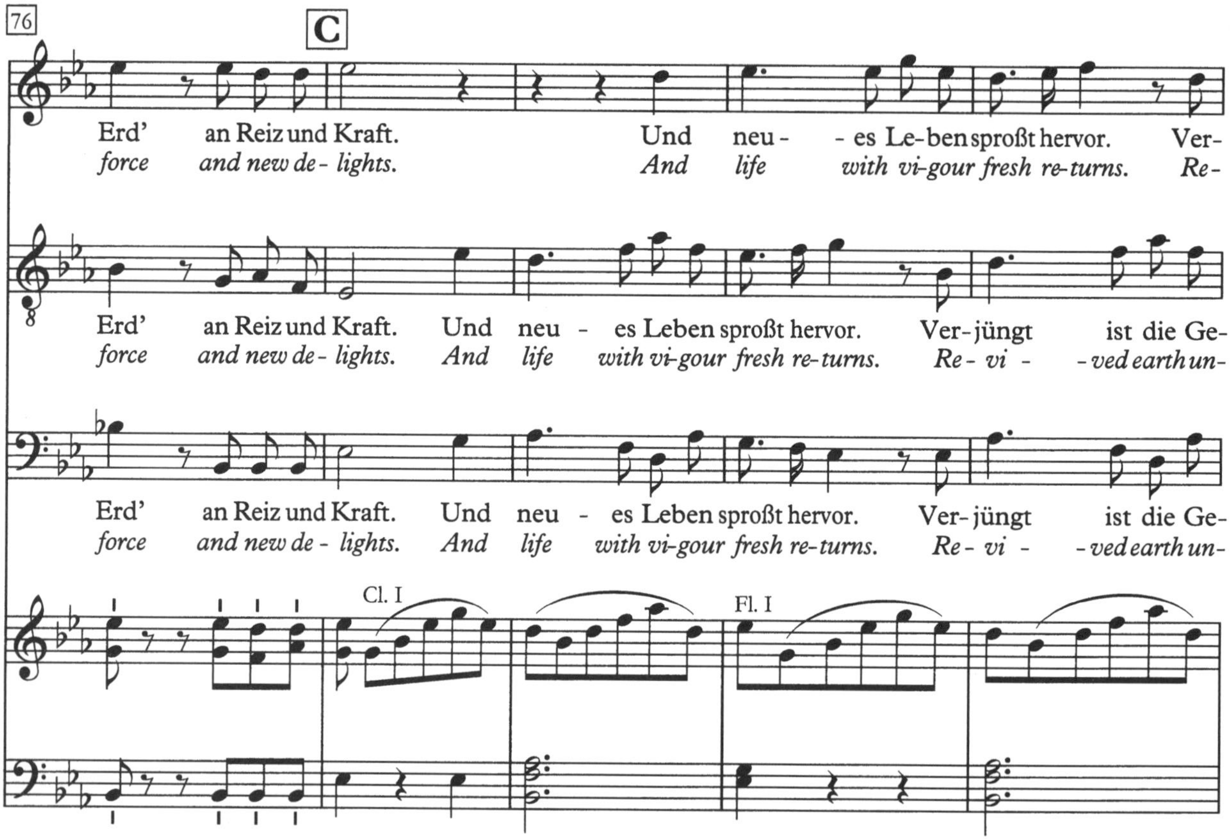
76
C
Erd' an Reiz und Kraft. Und neu - - es Le-ben sproßt hervor. Ver-
force and new de- lights. And life with vi-gour fresh re-turns. Re-
Erd' an Reiz und Kraft. Und neu - es Leben sproßt hervor. Ver-jüngt ist die Ge-
force and new de- lights. And life with vi-gour fresh re-turns. Re- vi - -ved earth un-
Erd' an Reiz und Kraft. Und neu - es Leben sproßt hervor. Ver-jüngt ist die Ge-
force and new de - lights. And life with vi-gour fresh re-turns. Re- vi - -ved earth un-
Cl. I
Fl. I

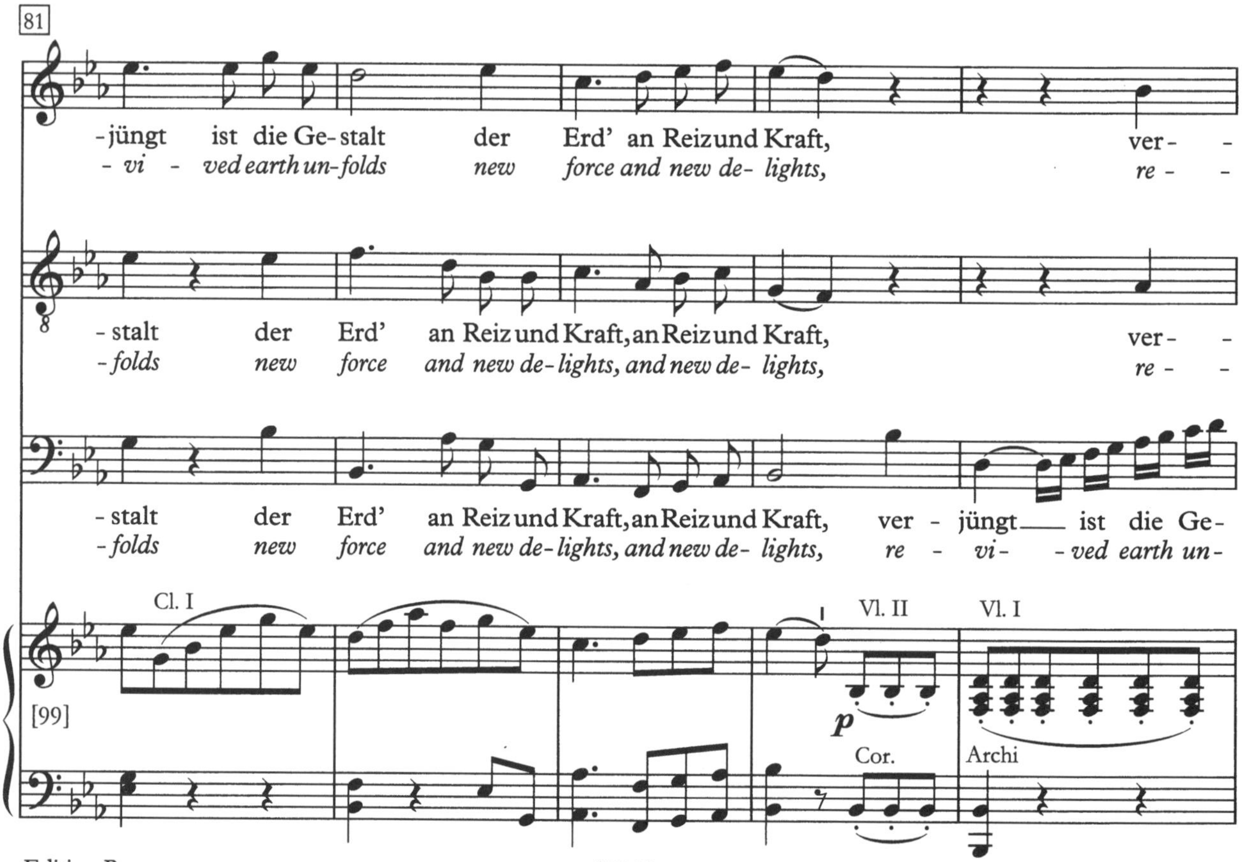
81
-jüngt ist die Ge-stalt der Erd' an Reiz und Kraft, ver- -
- vi - ved earth un-folds new force and new de- lights, re - -
- stalt der Erd' an Reiz und Kraft, an Reiz und Kraft, ver- -
- folds new force and new de- lights, and new de- lights, re - -
- stalt der Erd' an Reiz und Kraft, an Reiz und Kraft, ver - jüngt ist die Ge-
- folds new force and new de- lights, and new de- lights, re - vi- - ved earth un-
Cl. I
[99]
Vl. II
p
Cor.
Vl. I
Archi

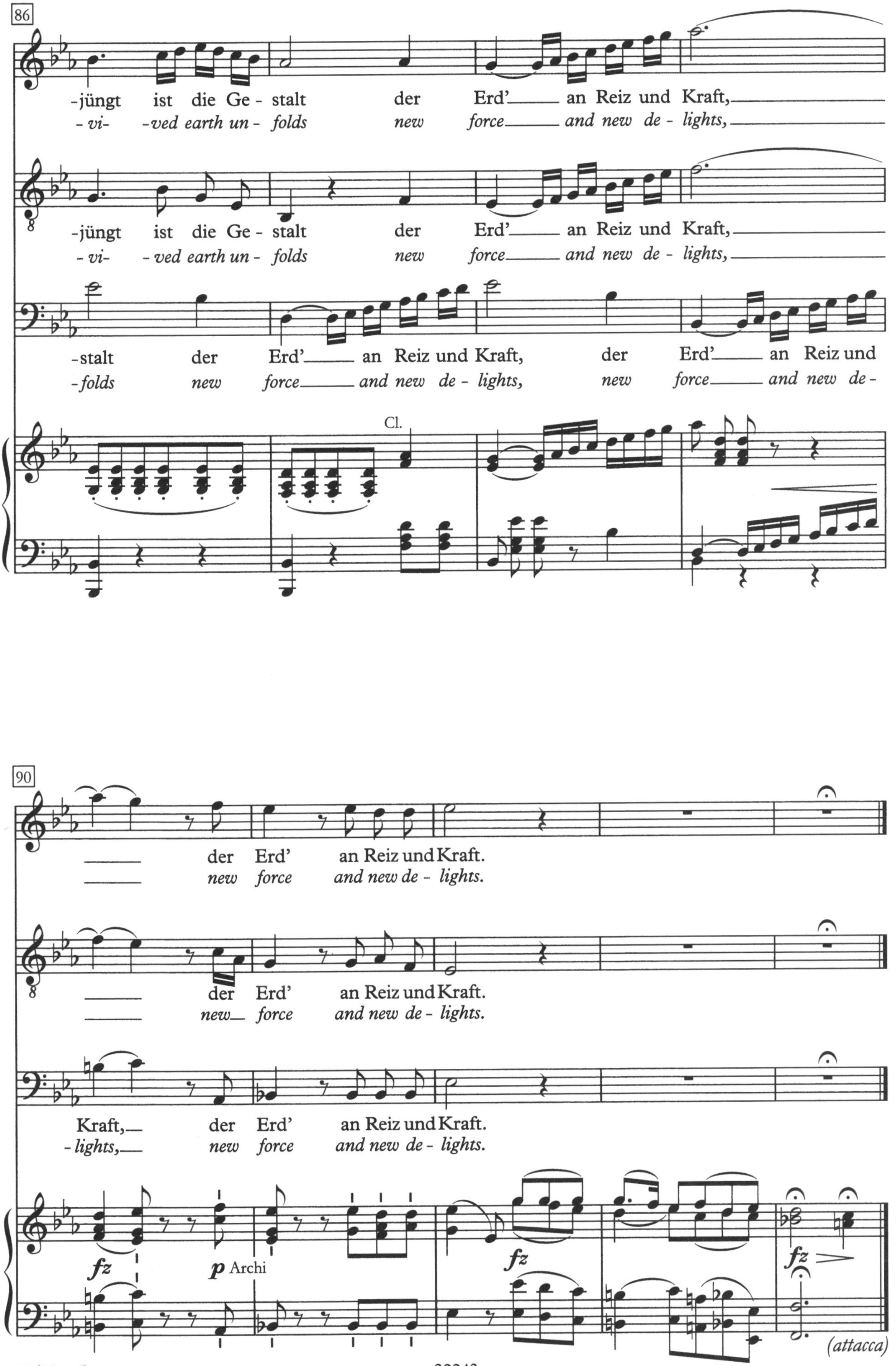
86
-jüngt ist die Ge - stalt der Erd' an Reiz und Kraft,
- vi- -ved earth un - folds new force and new de - lights,
-jüngt ist die Ge - stalt der Erd' an Reiz und Kraft,
- vi- - ved earth un - folds new force and new de - lights,
-stalt der Erd' an Reiz und Kraft, der Erd' an Reiz und
-folds new force and new de - lights, new force and new de-
Cl.
90
der Erd' an Reiz und Kraft.
new force and new de - lights.
der Erd' an Reiz und Kraft.
new force and new de - lights.
Kraft, der Erd' an Reiz und Kraft.
-lights, new force and new de - lights.
fz
p Archi
fz
fz
(attacca)

Teil III · Part III
Nr. 30 · No. 30
Rezitativ · Recitative

Nr. 31 · No. 31
Duett und Chor · Duet with Chorus

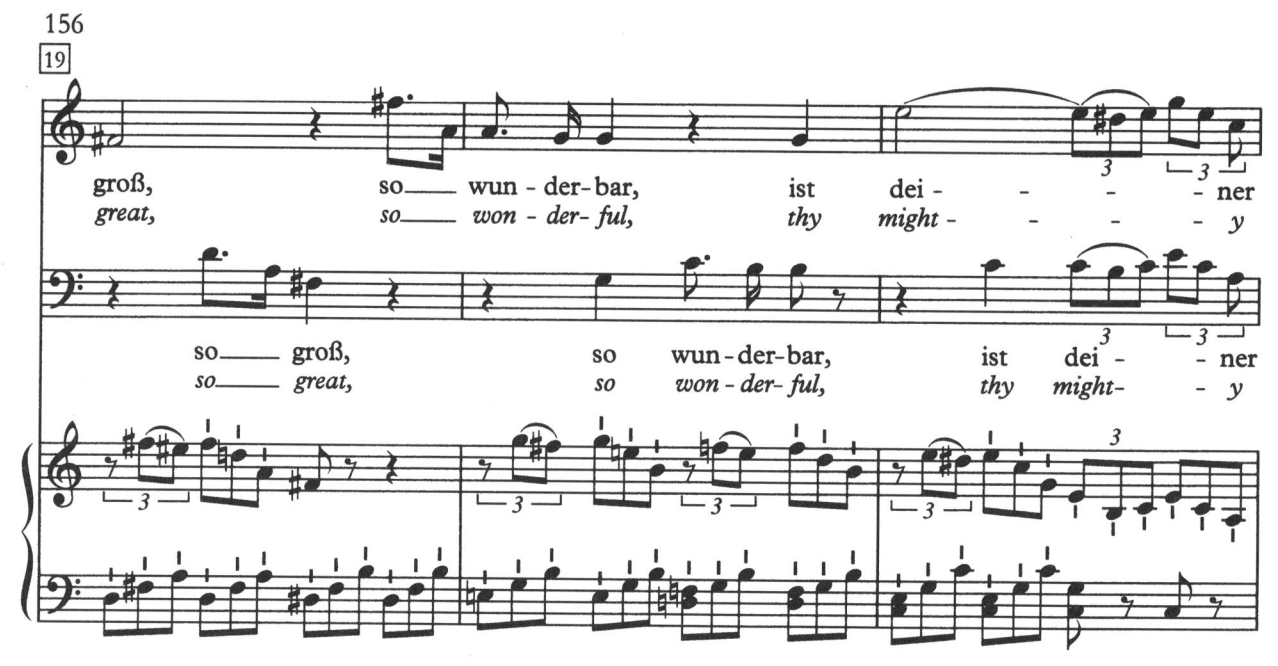

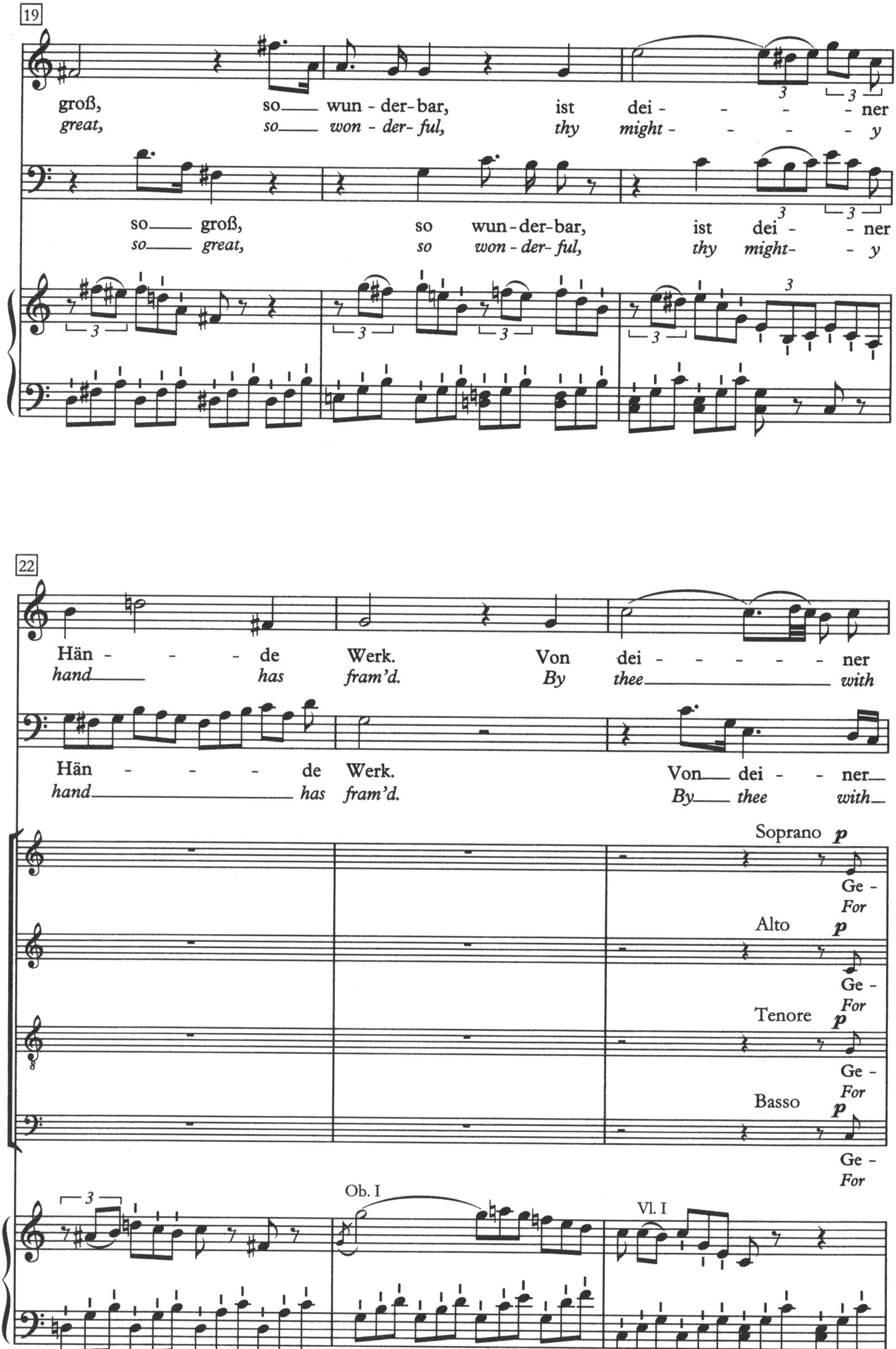
19
groß, so wun - der - bar, ist dei - - - - ner
great, so won - der - ful, thy might - - - - y
so groß, so wun - der - bar, ist dei - - ner
so great, so won - der - ful, thy might - - y
22
Hän - - - de Werk. Von dei - - - - - - ner
hand has fram'd. By thee with
Hän - - - de Werk. Von dei - - ner
hand has fram'd. By thee with
Soprano p
Ge -
For
Alto p
Ge -
For
Tenore p
Ge -
For
Basso p
Ge -
For
Ob. I
Vl. I

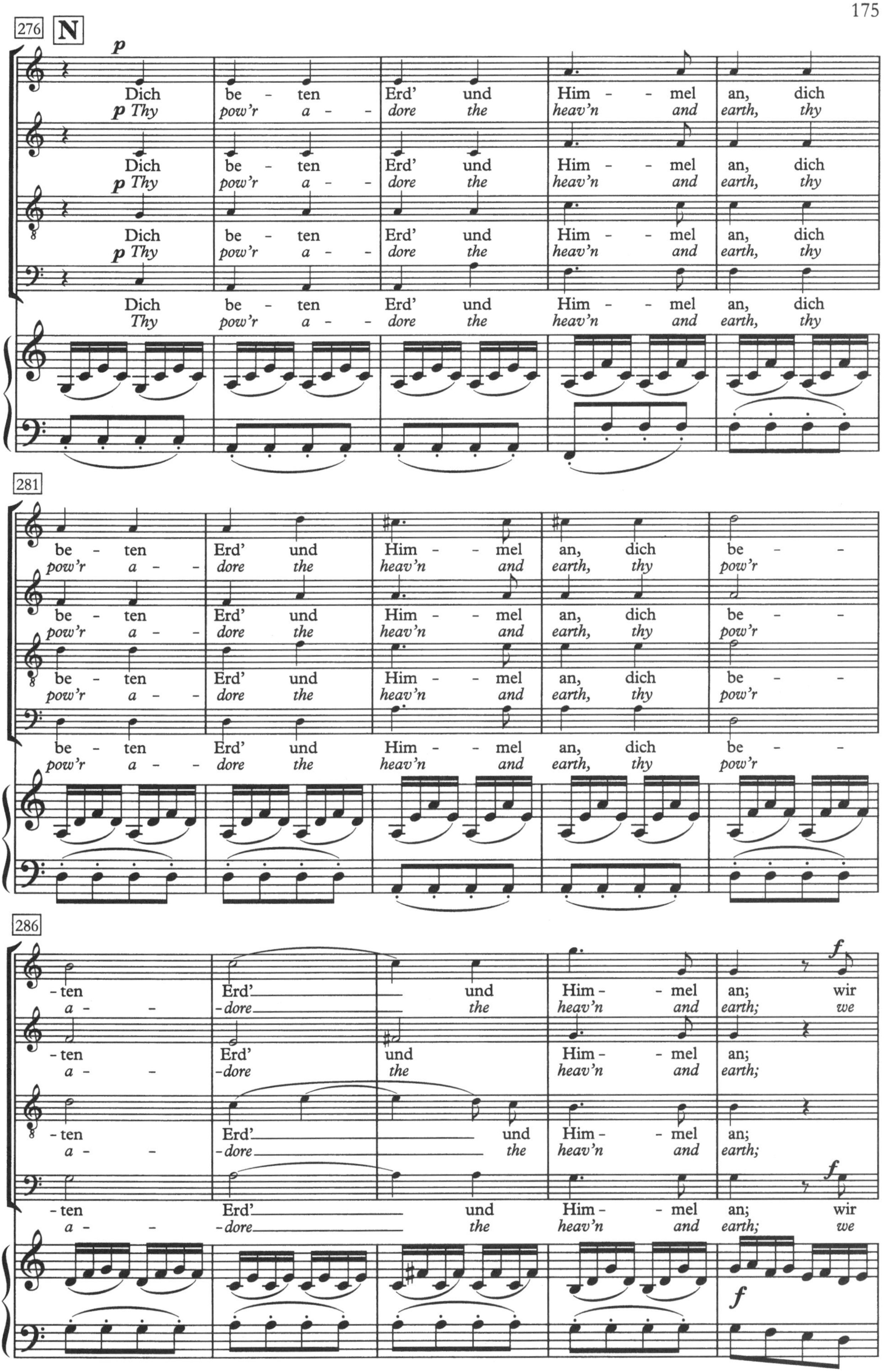
276
N
p
Dich be - ten Erd' und Him - mel an, dich
p Thy pow'r a - dore the heav'n and earth, thy
Dich be - ten Erd' und Him - mel an, dich
p Thy pow'r a - dore the heav'n and earth, thy
Dich be - ten Erd' und Him - mel an, dich
p Thy pow'r a - dore the heav'n and earth, thy
Dich be - ten Erd' und Him - mel an, dich
Thy pow'r a - dore the heav'n and earth, thy
281
be - ten Erd' und Him - mel an, dich be -
pow'r a - dore the heav'n and earth, thy pow'r
be - ten Erd' und Him - mel an, dich be -
pow'r a - dore the heav'n and earth, thy pow'r
be - ten Erd' und Him - mel an, dich be -
pow'r a - dore the heav'n and earth, thy pow'r
be - ten Erd' und Him - mel an, dich be -
pow'r a - dore the heav'n and earth, thy pow'r
286
- ten Erd' und Him - mel an; wir
a - - dore the heav'n and earth; we
f
- ten Erd' und Him - mel an;
a - - dore the heav'n and earth;
- ten Erd' und Him - mel an;
a - - dore the heav'n and earth;
- ten Erd' und Him - mel an; wir
a - - dore the heav'n and earth; we
f
f

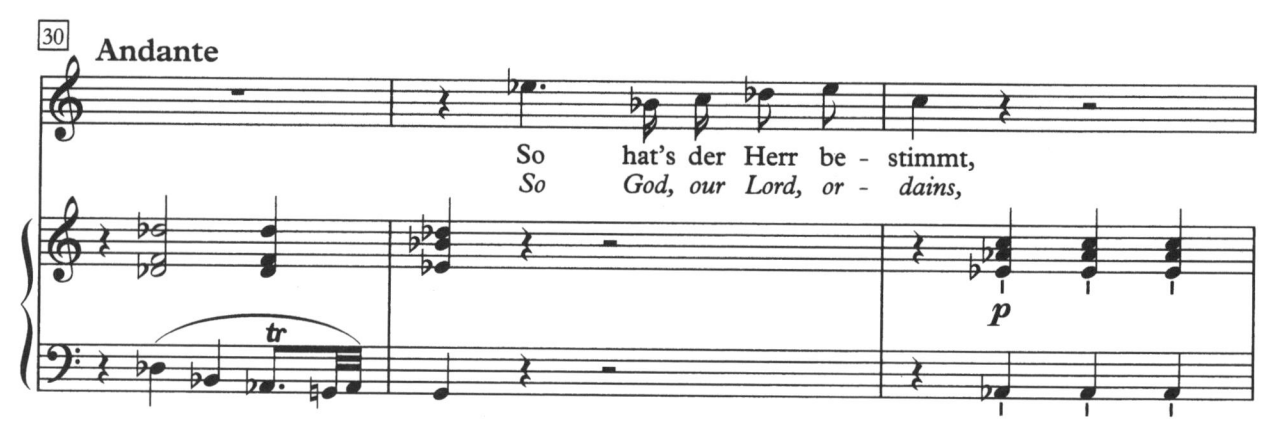

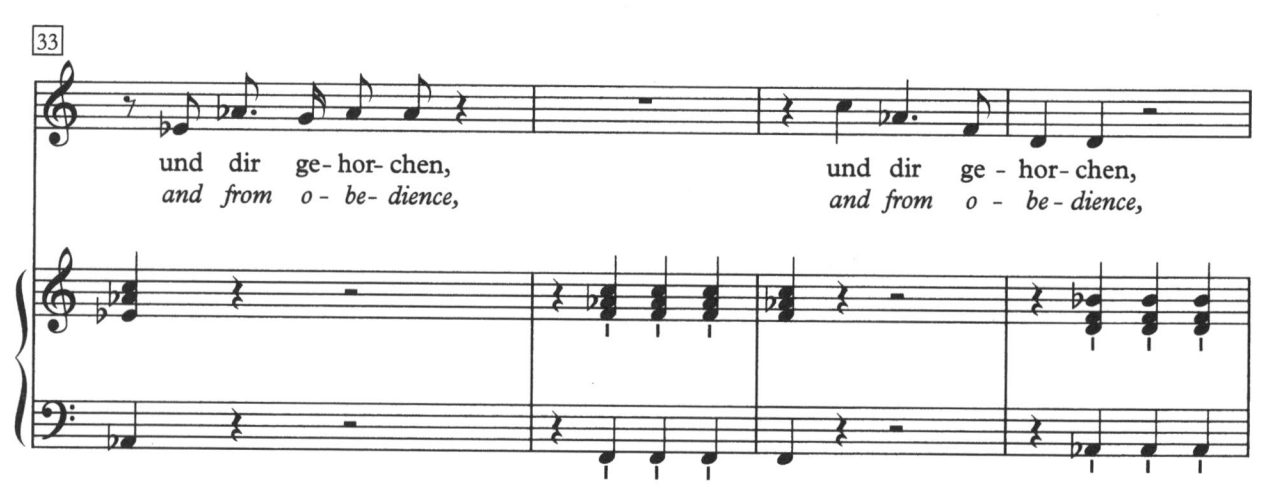

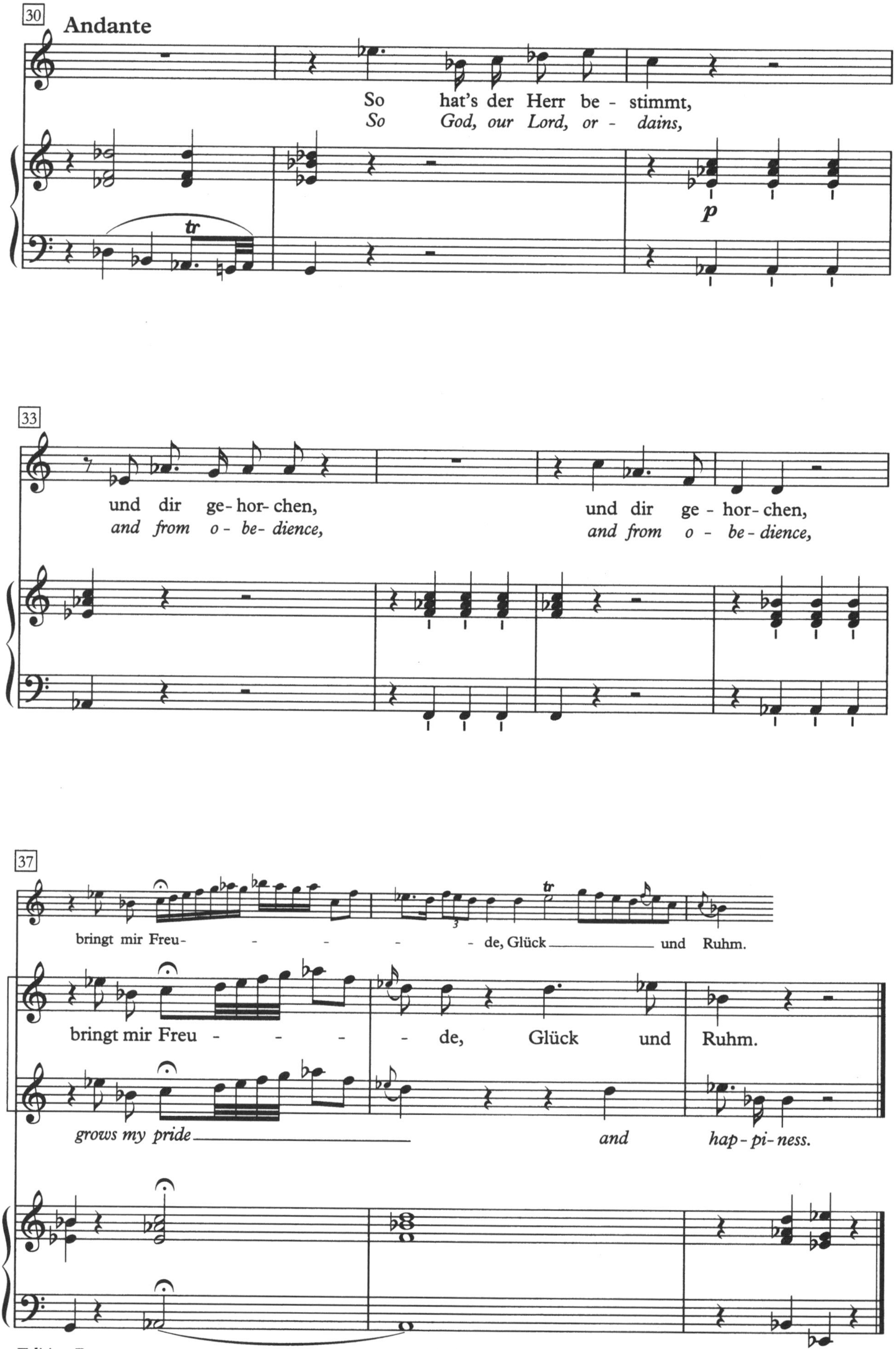
30
Andante
So hat's der Herr be - stimmt,
So God, our Lord, or - dains,
p
33
und dir ge-hor-chen,
and from o-be-dience,
und dir ge - hor-chen,
and from o - be-dience,
37
bringt mir Freu- - - - - de, Glück und Ruhm.
bringt mir Freu - - - de, Glück und Ruhm.
grows my pride and hap-pi-ness.

Nr. 33 · No. 33
Duett · Duet

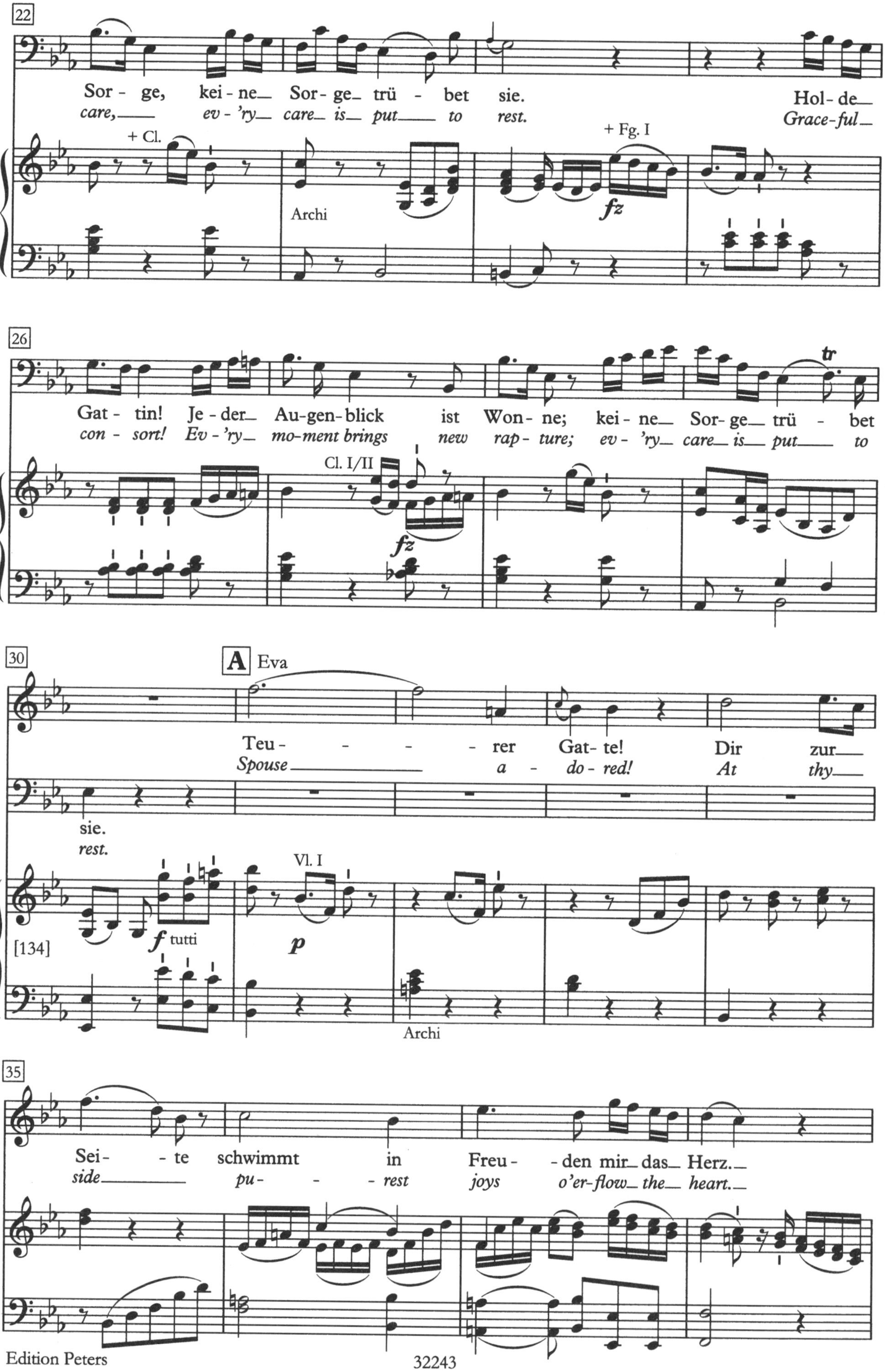
22
Sor- ge, kei- ne Sor- ge- trü - bet sie. Hol- de
care, ev- 'ry care is put to rest. Grace-ful
+ Cl.
Archi
+ Fg. I
fz
26
Gat - tin! Je - der Au-gen-blick ist Won - ne; kei - ne Sor- ge- trü - bet
con - sort! Ev - 'ry mo-ment brings new rap - ture; ev - 'ry care is put to
Cl. I/II
fz
tr
30
A Eva
Teu- - - - rer Gat- te! Dir zur
Spouse a - do-red! At thy
sie.
rest.
Vl. I
f tutti
[134]
p
Archi
35
Sei- - te schwimmt in Freu - den mir das Herz.
side pu- - - rest joys o'er-flow the heart.

Nr. 34 · No. 34
Rezitativ · Recitative

Nr. 35 · No. 35

Chor mit Soli · Chorus with Soli

206

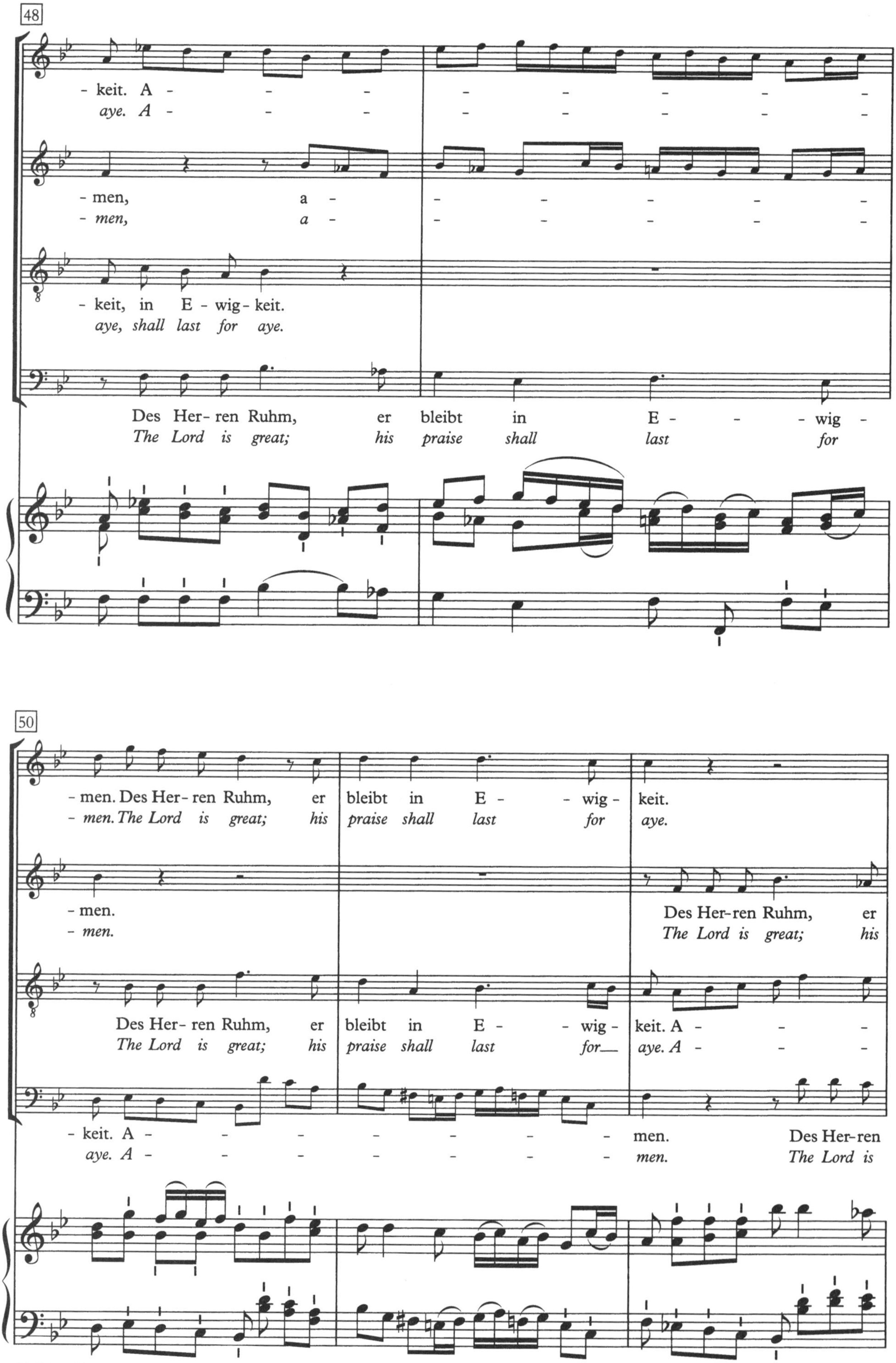
48
- keit. A - - - - - - - - -
aye. A - - - - - - - - -
- men, a - - - - - -
- men, a - - - - - -
- keit, in E - wig - keit.
aye, shall last for aye.
Des Her - ren Ruhm, er bleibt in E - - - wig -
The Lord is great; his praise shall last for
50
- men. Des Her - ren Ruhm, er bleibt in E - - wig - keit.
- men. The Lord is great; his praise shall last for aye.
- men.
- men.
Des Her - ren Ruhm, er
The Lord is great; his
Des Her - ren Ruhm, er bleibt in E - - wig - keit. A - - -
The Lord is great; his praise shall last for aye. A - - -
- keit. A - - - - - - - - men. Des Her - ren
aye. A - - - - - - - - men. The Lord is

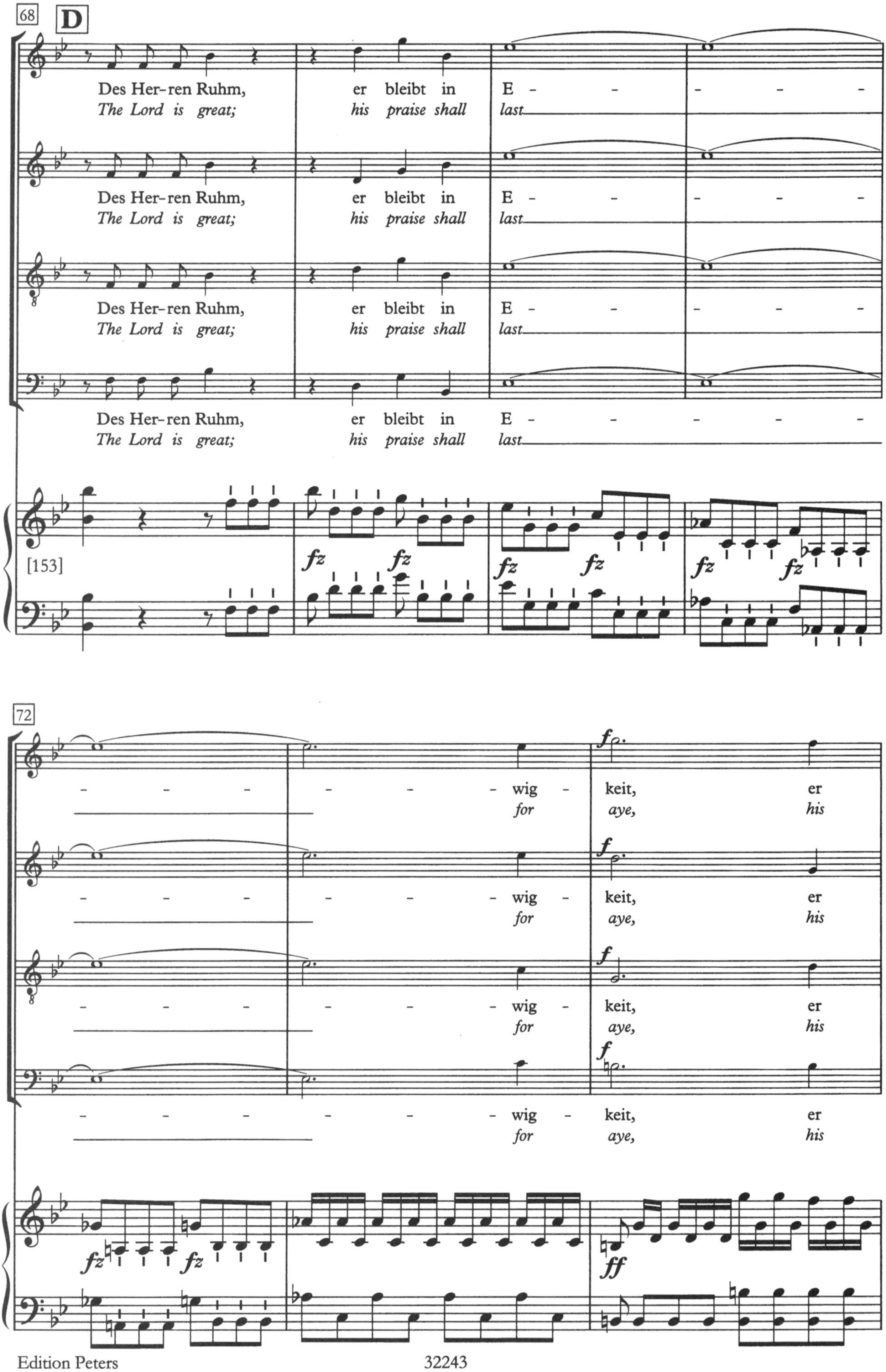
68
D
Des Her-ren Ruhm, er bleibt in E - - - - - -
The Lord is great; his praise shall last
[153]
fz
72
wig - keit, er
for aye, his
f
ff

Nachwort

Während seines ganzen Lebens legte Joseph Haydn (1732-1809) das Hauptgewicht seiner Arbeit auf das Gebiet der Instrumentalmusik: Im Zentrum standen Sinfonien, Streichquartette, Klavier- und Kammermusikwerke. Und dennoch komponierte er, wenngleich in weit geringerer Zahl, immer wieder auch Vokalwerke, die zwar nicht ausschließlich, aber doch meist für den Kirchenraum bestimmt waren. In der Zeit seit 1782 jedoch, als Kaiser Joseph II. vehement in die Souveränität der kirchlichen Autoritäten eingegriffen und eine Gottesdienstordnung erlassen hatte, die eine festliche, instrumentalbegleitete Musik weitgehend aus der Kirche verbannte, schwieg Haydn auf diesem Sektor. Dies betraf konkret die Jahre zwischen 1783 und 1796. Es darf als ein Wunder in der schöpferischen Biographie des Komponisten angesehen werden, dass nach Aufhebung des Erlasses der inzwischen 64-Jährige praktisch seine gesamte Schaffenskraft der Chormusik zuwandte und neue Großwerke vollbrachte, die dem schon vorhandenen Ruhm des Meisters nachgerade eine neue Dimension hinzufügten. Zwischen 1796 und 1802 sollten es die sechs großen Hochämter[1] werden, ferner *Die sieben letzten Worte unseres Erlösers am Kreuze* (in der Vokalfassung beendet spätestens Anfang 1796) und schließlich auch die großformatigen Oratorien *Die Schöpfung* (1796-98) und *Die Jahreszeiten* (fertiggestellt 1801); letztere waren keinesfalls für den kirchlichen Gebrauch bestimmt, aber ebenso wie Händels Oratorien dennoch geeignet, im sakralen Raum aufgeführt zu werden.

Zu Beginn der 1790er Jahre hatte Haydn zwei Konzertreisen nach England unternommen und war 1795 von seinem zweiten, höchst erfolgreich abgeschlossenen Aufenthalt endgültig nach Wien zurückgekehrt. In früheren Jahren war es niemals zu größeren Reisen gekommen, und Haydns arbeitsreiches Leben hatte sich mehr oder weniger zwischen Esterház, dem Sitz seiner Brotherren, und Wien abgespielt. Doch dann war er mit knapp 58 Jahren im Dezember 1790 einer bereits mehrfach ausgesprochenen Einladung des seit 1781 in London ansässigen Geigers und Konzertveranstalters Johann Peter Salomon (1745-1816) gefolgt, in England eigene Konzerte zu leiten. Diese Möglichkeit hatte sich überhaupt erst ergeben, nachdem Haydns Dienstherr, Fürst Nicolaus I. (der „Prächtige" oder „Prachtliebende"), im September gestorben war und dessen Nachfolger, Anton, die Esterházysche Kapelle (bis auf die Bläser für die Jagd) aufgelöst und ihren Leiter mit einer vergleichsweise bescheidenen Pension abgefunden hatte.[2]

So kam Haydn recht plötzlich in eine andere, ihm fremde Welt und erlebte in London ein öffentliches Musikleben, wie man es in Wien nicht kannte. Allein die Tatsache, dass während seiner ersten Saison fünf verschiedene Subskriptionsserien einem breit gefächerten Publikum angeboten wurden, wird ihn nachhaltig berührt haben. Er besuchte selbst mehrere Konzerte und war begeistert von der Qualität der Aufführungen. Und seine eigenen Konzerte wurden zu glänzenden Erfolgen, ja zu wahren Triumphen, die sein Selbstgefühl außerordentlich gesteigert haben dürften. So unternahm er 1794, wieder für zwei Konzertsaisons, eine zweite Reise, hatte erneut große Erfolge und kehrte voller neuer Eindrücke zurück. Wen sollte es da verwundern, dass solche Erlebnisse einschneidend auf sein weiteres Leben und Schaffen wirkten?

Schon während seiner ersten Englandreise 1791 hatte Haydn in der Westminster-Abtei Aufführungen Händelscher Oratorien während der großen Händel-Gedächtnisfeier erlebt und die gewaltige Klangwirkung von einem riesigen Aufgebot an Mitwirkenden bestaunt. 885 Personen sollen beteiligt gewesen sein, wie Haydn in seinen eigenen Notizen festhielt, andere Quellen sprechen sogar von erheblich mehr Akteuren.[3] Dieses Ereignis hat in Haydn zweifellos einen tiefen Eindruck hinterlassen, und er wird schon bald mit dem Gedanken gespielt haben, sich selbst einer solchen Aufgabe, gemessen an Händels *Messias*, zu stellen. Der Überlieferung zufolge hat Salomon ihm ein Textbuch über die biblische Schöpfungsgeschichte gegeben, das ein Mann namens Lidley ein halbes Jahrhundert zuvor für Händel verfasst haben soll.[4] Dieses Libretto (nach John Miltons Epos *Paradise Lost*) gelangte durch Haydn an Baron Gottfried van Swieten (1733-1803), Präfekt an der Kaiserlichen Hofbibliothek in Wien und Geschäftsführer einer Gesellschaft hochadliger Musikliebhaber, der „Associrten H.[errn] Cavaliers"[5]. Van Swieten gab dem Textbuch eine neue Fasson, übersetzte es ins Deutsche und nannte es *Die Schöpfung*. „Der Antheil, den ich an dem ursprünglich englischen Werk habe" – berichtete van Swieten der *Allgemeinen Musikalischen Zeitung* –, „ist zwar etwas mehr als bloße Uebersetzung, doch bei weiten [sic] nicht so beschaffen, daß ich es als mein ansehen könnte."[6] Da sich Lidleys Textbuch, die Grundlage für van Swietens Arbeit, nicht erhalten hat, konnte dessen Eigenanteil an der deutschen Übersetzung nie verlässlich bestimmt werden. Auch ließen einige sprachliche Schwächen im englischen Text schon bald und später wiederholt den Verdacht aufkommen, van Swieten habe seiner deutschen Übersetzung nicht den originalen englischen Text zur Seite gestellt, sondern eine eigene Rückübersetzung seiner deutschen Fassung ins Englische. In der Folge versuchte man sich in (bisweilen fragwürdigen) sprachlichen Verbesserungen und musste dabei naturgemäß auch einige Eingriffe in die musikalische Diktion in Kauf nehmen. Heute wissen wir, dass van Swietens englische Sprachkenntnisse nicht ausgereicht haben, ein ganzes Textbuch in die ihm eher fremde Sprache zu übersetzen. Als ebenso sicher gilt, dass Haydn einen deutschsprachigen Text vertonte, den van Swieten aus dem Englischen gewonnen und bestenfalls um einige Zusätze aus der eigenen Feder erweitert hatte. Den englischen Text passte van Swieten der fertigen Komposition dann erst in einem weiteren Schritt an.[7] Und so soll diese englische Fassung, trotz mancher Unzulänglichkeiten, in der Neuausgabe weitgehend unangetastet bleiben, abgesehen von einigen wenigen Korrekturen, die im Revisionsbericht der Partiturausgabe ausgewiesen sind.[8]

Doch van Swieten wirkte nicht nur als Übersetzer, sondern Haydn hatte in ihm einen Mitstreiter gefunden, der in einer freien Bearbeitung erst ein wirkungsvolles Libretto herstellte und zusätzlich detaillierte Anregungen zur musikalischen Umsetzung gab, die Haydn durchaus zu schätzen wusste. Durch den präzisen Zuschnitt des Textes werde, so der Komponist in anderem Zusammenhang, *„die Arbeit des Compositeurs erleichtert, und der Dichter sey genöthiget musicalisch zu dichten"*[9]. Und schließlich garantierte van Swieten zusammen mit adligen Freunden, den Assoziierten Kavalieren, die Aufführungskosten und ein angemessenes Honorar für Haydn. Dabei handelte es sich um ein Honorar, wie es vorher noch niemals einem Komponisten gezahlt wurde: 500 Dukaten, was bedeutete, dass Haydn etwa das Fünffache dessen erhielt, was damals üblicherweise für eine Oper gezahlt zu werden pflegte.[10] Die erste Aufführung fand demzufolge im privaten Rahmen vor einem adligen Publikum und eigens geladenen Gästen im Wiener Palais des Fürsten Schwarzenberg (1893 abgetragen) am Neuen Markt (heute Mehlmarkt) statt. Dies geschah am 29. April 1798, eine Wiederholung folgte am nächsten Tag. Die erste öffentliche Aufführung sollte jedoch erst ein volles Jahr später im alten Burgtheater zustande kommen: am 19. März 1799, Joseph Haydns Namenstag. Haydn dirigierte diese ersten Aufführungen selbst. Manche Berichte von Zeitzeugen sind überliefert, und alle vermelden übereinstimmend einen überaus großen Erfolg: „*Die Musik hat eine Kraft der Darstellung, welche alle Vorstellung übertrif[f]t; man wird hingerissen, sieht der Elemente Sturm, sieht es Licht werden, die gefallenen Geister tief in den Abgrund sinken, zittert beym Rollen des Donners, stimmt mit in den Feyergesang der himmlischen Bewohner. Die Sonne steigt, der Vögel frohes Lob begrüßt die steigende; der Pflanzen Grün entkeimt dem Boden, es rieselt silbern der kühle Bach, und vom Meeresgrunde auf schäumender Woge wälzt sich Leviathan empor. ... Schon sind drey Tage seit dem glücklichen Abende verflossen, und noch klingt es in meinen Ohren, in meinem Herzen; noch engt der Empfindungen Menge selbst bey der Erinnerung die Brust mir.*"[11]

Haydn leitete etliche Aufführungen der *Schöpfung* bis 1802 oder 1803 selbst, darunter sogar eine in Budapest (8. März 1800). Dazu zählen – neben anderen – die ersten Privataufführungen im Wiener Schwarzenberg-Palais ebenso wie mehrere Wiederholungsveranstaltungen an demselben Ort (im Mai des Jahres und März des Folgejahres), oder die ersten öffentlichen Aufführungen im Burgtheater und das von der Wiener Tonkünstler-Sozietät am 22./23. Dezember 1799 initiierte Konzert, ebenfalls im Burgtheater. Alle diese Aufführungen, zumindest solange aus dem einmal erstellten Material gespielt wurde, sind für die quellenkritische Untersuchung und für aufführungspraktische Hinweise von besonderer Bedeutung.[12] Denn Haydn hat immer wieder kleinere Korrekturen veranlasst, teils selbst im Notenmaterial notiert, wie eigenhändige Eintragungen zeigen, teils möglicherweise auch nur angesagt, worauf Notizen von fremder Hand verweisen können.

Die Haydn-Forschung hat viele Belege zusammengetragen über die ersten Aufführungen und in diesem Zusammenhang auch über die sehr unterschiedliche Besetzungsstärke von Orchester und Chor.[13] Daraus wird ersichtlich, dass es sowohl minimal besetzte Aufführungen als auch Orchesterstärken von bis zu ca. 200 Musikern gegeben hat.[14]

Haydn hatte die Absicht, einen Partiturdruck im Selbstverlag herauszubringen, anstatt ihn einem der Wiener Musikverlage oder beispielsweise Breitkopf & Härtel in Leipzig anzubieten, obwohl dorthin bereits gute Beziehungen über den Wiener Verlagsagenten, den sächsischen Diplomaten Georg August Griesinger (gest. 1828), bestanden. So veröffentlichte Haydn im Juni 1799 einen Subskriptionsaufruf in einigen wichtigen Zeitungen: in der *Wiener Zeitung* (17.6.1799) und in der *Allgemeinen Musikalischen Zeitung* (26.6.1799, *Intelligenzblatt* Nr. XV). Einer Anzeige des mit dem Vertrieb beauftragten Verlegers Artaria (*Wiener Zeitung* vom 26.2.1800) zufolge lag die Partitur Ende Februar 1800 im Druck vor. Erst nach längeren Verhandlungen verkaufte Haydn 1803 die Stichplatten an Breitkopf & Härtel, Leipzig. Mit neuer Firmierung erschien die Partitur in vielen Plattenabzügen bis 1871, als ein Neustich notwendig wurde. Dass bis dahin immer wieder Platten wegen hoher Abnutzung nachgestochen werden mussten, erscheint selbstverständlich und ist auch belegbar.

Der von Haydn selbst herausgegebene Originaldruck diente lange Zeit als Vorlage für spätere Druckausgaben verschiedener Verlage, so auch für den bei C. F. Peters 1871 herausgegebenen Neustich.[15] Dort sind im Rahmen eines Vorwortes zwar einige Änderungen gegenüber der Vorlage benannt, doch darüber hinaus auch mancherlei „Verbesserungen" aus dem damaligen Musikverständnis heraus stillschweigend eingebracht worden. Das betrifft vor allem Ergänzungen von Artikulationszeichen, mit der Folge einer Nivellierung der ursprünglichen, vermutlich sogar absichtsvollen Unterscheidungen zu Parallelstellen.

Die vorliegende Neuausgabe erkennt in Haydns Erstdruck einen hohen Quellenwert, zumal der Komponist nicht nur die Stichvorlage durchgesehen hat, wie eigenhändige Eintragungen belegen, sondern auch bei der Korrektur beteiligt gewesen sein dürfte, da es einige Änderungen gegenüber der Stichvorlage gegeben hat, die kaum auf eigenmächtige Verbesserungen anderer Beteiligter (van Swietens oder gar der Notenstecher) zurückzuführen sind.

Haydn hat die einzelnen Sätze nicht nummeriert. Die dreiteilige Gliederung hingegen ist authentisch. So erschien auch der Originaldruck ohne Nummern. In der Stichvorlage wurde – vermutlich zu einem viel späteren Zeitpunkt – eine bis 34 fortlaufende Nummerierung nachgetragen, die der Zählung in der alten Peters-Partiturausgabe genau entspricht und wahrscheinlich sogar auf dieser beruht. Spätere Generationen haben immer wieder versucht, eine eigene Nummerierung einzuführen und sind dabei zu sehr unterschiedlichen Ergebnissen gelangt. Entgegen manch anders lautender Separierung der einzelnen Satz-Teile wurde in der jetzigen Neuausgabe die ältere Peters-Einteilung mit einer einzigen Einschränkung beibehalten: Das Rezitativ des Raphael („Im Anfange schuf Gott Himmel und Erde") aus der alten Nr. 1 wurde herausgelöst und als Nr. 2 verselbständigt. Hier folgen wir dem Vorbild des von Eusebius Mandyczewski herausgegebenen (alten) Gesamtausgaben-Bandes (Breitkopf & Härtel, 1924).[16] So ergibt sich für die hier vorgelegte Neuausgabe eine Zählung bis Nr. 35.[17]

Bei Aufführungen der späten Vokalwerke Haydns stellt sich immer wieder die Frage nach der Notwendigkeit von nicht eigens notierten Auszierungen – Ornamenten und Melismen –, da bekannt ist, dass Haydn kein großer Freund von Sängerwillkürlichkeiten war.[18] Allerdings lobte Haydn die Sopranistin Therese Fischer – mitgeteilt von Albert Christoph Dies in einem Bericht über die Aufführung der *Schöpfung* im März 1808, den letzten öffentlichen Auftritt Haydns –, „*sie hätte ihre Stimme mit der möglichsten Zierlichkeit und so treu gesungen, daß sie sich nicht den geringsten unzweckmäßigen Zusatz erlaubt hätte.*"[19] Daraus ist mit einiger Sicherheit abzuleiten, dass Haydn gegen passende Verzierungen in angemessener Ausführung nichts einzuwenden hatte. Und so finden sich auch in den Uraufführungsstimmen und in einem weiteren Material aus Haydns Nachlass verschiedene Auszierungsvarianten für die Solostimmen. Da nicht sicher bestimmt werden kann, von wann diese datieren, sollten wir durchaus davon ausgehen, dass sie erst in wesentlich späterer Zeit eingetragen wurden, Haydn sie also nicht gekannt haben wird. Dennoch geben sie einen gewissen Anhalt für eine gewachsene Traditionslinie. In der Neuausgabe wurden sie im Kleinstich beigefügt. Sie sollen mit aller Vorsicht zum gefälligen Gebrauch anregen.

Haydn selbst verwendete meist nur vier Verzierungssymbole: das normale Trillerzeichen (*tr*), das Zeichen für einen Pralltriller (⌒), den sogenannten Doppelschlag (∞) und ein Zeichen, das er selbst „*Halb Mordent*" (⊬)[20] nannte. In den Quellen begegnen wir allerdings vielen Unklarheiten über die rechte Darstellung des jeweiligen Ornaments, doch wurde so weit als möglich versucht, entsprechende Unterscheidungen zu klären und in der Neuausgabe zu platzieren.

Die Neuausgabe folgt den Regeln der heutigen Editionspraxis. Besondere Beachtung galt der Notierungsform von Vorschlagsnötchen. Der Herausgeber entschied sich (wo notwendig auch gegen die Quellen) für die Praxis der sogenannten „Halbwertnotierung", wie sie Haydn zwar zeitweilig, im Alter aber keineswegs konsequent angewendet hat, indem er oftmals – unabhängig vom Wert der Hauptnoten – Achtelnötchen notierte. In der Neuausgabe wurde jedoch für die kleinste Werteinheit der Vorschlagsnoten die Sechzehntel (auch vor 16tel-Noten und kleineren Werten) beibehalten, unabhängig von der spielpraktischen Ausführung (kurzer oder langer Vorschlag).

Die Ausgabe folgt in der Notierung von Artikulationszeichen dem Befund der jeweils maßgeblichen Quelle. Der Unterscheidung von Staccatopunkten und -strichen (letztere sind in ihrer gelegentlichen Doppeldeutigkeit durchaus auch als Betonungszeichen zu verstehen) wurde größter Wert beigemessen. Fragwürdige resp. völlig abweichende Lesarten sind im Revisionsbericht der Partitur kommentiert. Ergänzungen des Herausgebers wurden grundsätzlich sehr sparsam vorgenommen, auch wurde vermieden, mechanisch anzugleichen, um der Gefahr einer Nivellierung zu entgehen. So bleiben den Ausführenden genügend Möglichkeiten für eine eigenständige Interpretation, zumal sehr oft die vorhandenen Artikulationszeichen lediglich eine Linie andeuten und nicht immer eine entsprechend konsequente Weiterführung verlangen.

Der vorliegende Klavierauszug orientiert sich in vielen Einzelheiten an der alten Ausgabe aus dem Jahre 1800 von August Eberhard Müller (1767-1817), ohne diese allerdings vollständig zu übernehmen. Der Klavierauszug des Leipziger Thomaskantors (1804-10) und nachmaligen Weimarer Hofkapellmeisters war eine von vier Konkurrenzausgaben, die im selben Jahr kurz nacheinander veröffentlicht wurden.[21] Noch bevor überhaupt die Partitur der *Schöpfung* gedruckt werden konnte, wurde in Wien bereits ein Klavierauszug angekündigt (Mollo 1799). Über diesen soll sich Haydn sehr geärgert und ihn als „elendes Machwerk" bezeichnet haben.[22] Dem Klavierauszug Müllers hingegen stellte kein geringerer als Haydn selbst das schöne Zeugnis aus, er sei *„der beste, verständlichste und leichteste unter seinen Brüdern".*[23]

Klaus Burmeister

---

[1] Es waren dies die *Paukenmesse* (Hob. XXII: 9), die *Heiligmesse* (Nr. 10), die *Nelsonmesse* (Nr. 11), die *Theresienmesse* (Nr. 12), die *Schöpfungsmesse* (Nr. 13) und die *Harmoniemesse* (Nr. 14). Haydn komponierte diese Werke im Auftrage seines letzten Dienstherrn, Nicolaus II., gedacht als Aufmerksamkeit des Fürsten zum Namensfeste seiner Gattin, Josepha Hermenegild.

[2] Nachdem auch Fürst Anton gestorben war (22.1.1794), rief sein Sohn, Nicolaus II., nach Rückkehr Haydns von seiner zweiten Englandreise die Kapelle wieder zusammen und übertrug Haydn nominell die Leitung, u.a. mit der Aufgabe, jährlich eine Messe zu komponieren (s. Anm. 1).

[3] Haydn notierte die Zahl „885" in seinen beiden sogenannten Londoner Notizbüchern; s. Dénes Bartha (Hg.), *Joseph Haydn, Gesammelte Briefe und Aufzeichnungen*, Kassel 1965, S. 485 u. 506. Bei C. F. Pohl z.B. (*Haydn in London*, Wien 1867, S. 136) ist die Rede von über 1000 Mitwirkenden.

[4] Georg August Griesinger, *Biographische Notizen über Joseph Haydn*, Leipzig 1810, Neuausgabe Leipzig 1975, S. 51. Der bei Griesinger mitgeteilte Name Lidley lässt sich in keiner anderen Quelle nachweisen. Obwohl im Laufe der Zeit verschiedene Verfasser in Betracht gezogen wurden, ist die Autorschaft des englischen Textes bis heute ungeklärt. Textvergleiche haben gezeigt, dass die englische Vorlage zumindest auf einer Überlieferung von Miltons *Paradise Lost* beruht.

[5] Diese „*Associrten H. Cavaliers*", so Haydn in einem Brief an Griesinger vom 3.7.1801 (Bartha, wie Anm. 3, S. 368f.), bildeten *„eine Gesellschaft von Freunden der Tonkunst ..., die aus einer kleinen Anzahl von Mitgliedern besteht, und jährlich einige Akademien zu veranstalten pflegte"* (zit. aus einem Bericht von Griesinger, in: *Allgemeine Musikalische Zeitung*, 20.5.1801. Genannt werden dort die Namen *„Lichtenstein, Esterhazy, Schwarzenberg, Auersperg, Lobkowitz, Lichnowsky, Trautmannsdorff, Swieten, Czernin, Fries, Aponi, Sinzendorf, Kinsky, Erdödy, Harrach").* Bereits seit 1786 veranstalteten und finanzierten die „*Cavaliers*" Aufführungen großer Vokalwerke, u.a. von J. A. Hasse, C. Ph. E. Bach, G. F. Händel (so auch die bekannten Bearbeitungen Mozarts).

[6] Zit. nach einem Brief van Swietens, in: *AMZ* I, Nr. 16 (3.1.1799).

[7] Vgl. Nicholas Temperley, *New Light on the Libretto of The Creation*, in: *Music in Eighteenth-Century England*, hg. von Christopher Hogwood und Richard Luckett, Cambridge 1983, S. 189–211.

[8] Die englische Textfassung ist nicht im ursprünglichen Aufführungsmaterial enthalten, dafür aber in einer Partiturabschrift, die aus Haydns Nachlass stammt und in der Berliner Staatsbibliothek – Preußischer Kulturbesitz aufbewahrt wird, ferner in der Stichvorlage und in Haydns Originaldruck (genaue Quellenbeschreibung im Revisionsbericht der Partitur).

[9] Brief Griesingers vom 21.4.1802, zit. nach Günter Thomas (Hg.), *Griesingers Briefe über Haydn*, in: *Haydn-Studien*, Bd. I, 2. Heft, München-Duisburg 1966, S. 89.

[10] 500 Dukaten entsprachen 2250 Gulden. Setzt man das Jahresgehalt eines Schullehrers von maximal 250 Gulden dagegen oder Haydns eigenes Jahresgehalt von 1700 Gulden, das er 1797 als Esterházyscher Kapellmeister erhielt, kann man den hohen Wert seines Honorars ermessen.

[11] Aus dem Bericht vom 3.5.1798, vermutlich von Friedrich Joseph Freiherr von Retzer verfasst, abgedruckt in: *Der neue Teutsche Merkur*, hg. von C. M. Wieland, Weimar 1798, *6. Stück. Jun. 1798, Zweyter Band*, S. 190.

[12] Das von Haydn für seine eigenen Aufführungen benutzte Material (Partiturabschrift und Stimmen) gelangte aus dem Besitz der Wiener Tonkünstler-Sozietät in die Wiener Stadt- und Landesbibliothek und liegt – neben anderen Quellen – dieser Neuausgabe zugrunde.

[13] Vgl. A. Peter Brown, *Performing Haydn's The Creation: Reconstruction of the Earliest Renditions*, Bloomington, Ind., 1986; Georg Feder, *Joseph Haydn, Die Schöpfung*, Kassel, Basel u.a. 1999.

[14] Haydn selbst hielt eine große Besetzung für die einzig angemessene: *„Meine Composition ist gros geschrieben, sagte er, sie wird daher auch nur bey einem zahlreichen und wohlgeübten Orchester ihr Glück und den gehörigen Effekt machen"* (so in Griesingers Brief vom 5.2.1800 an Breitkopf & Härtel, in: Otto Biba, *„Eben komme ich von Haydn ..." Georg August Griesingers Korrespondenz mit Joseph Haydns Verleger Breitkopf & Härtel 1799-1819*, Zürich 1987).

[15] Editionsnummer (EP) 1029, Plattennummer 5453.

[16] *Joseph Haydns Werke. Erste kritisch durchgesehene Gesamtausgabe. Serie 16. Kantaten und Oratorien. Band V. Die Schöpfung. Mit Vorwort und Revisionsbericht von E. Mandyczewski. Gestützt auf die Originalausgabe, aber nur mit deutschem Text*, Breitkopf & Härtel, Leipzig (1924); auch Breitkopf & Härtel's Partitur-Bibliothek, Nr. 4381.

[17] Die Breitkopf-Ausgaben zählen aufgrund einer anderen Unterteilung nur bis Nr. 32.

[18] Der Haydn-Biograph Giuseppe Carpani vertrat sogar die Meinung, die Solo-Partien sollten *„mit Einfachheit, Genauigkeit, Ausdruck und Portamento, aber ohne zu verzieren ausgeführt werden"* (*Le Haydine ovvero lettre su la vita e le opere del celebre maestro Giuseppe Haydn*, Mailand 1812, S. 182).

[19] Albert Christoph Dies, *Biographische Nachrichten von Joseph Haydn*, Wien 1810; Neuausgabe von Horst Seeger, Berlin 1959, ⁴1976, S. 175.

[20] In einem Brief vom 20.7.1781 an Artaria hat Haydn die vier *„Musicalischen Zeichen"* dargestellt, in einem anderen Brief an den Verleger vom 10.12.1785 ausdrücklich auf den „Halb Mordent" verwiesen. (Bartha, wie Anm. 3, S. 101 u. 148).

[21] Die 1800 erschienenen Klavierauszüge stammten vom Haydn-Schüler Sigismund Ritter von Neukomm (Artaria Wien), von Anton André, dem Sohn und Nachfolger des seinerzeit bereits bekannten Musikverlegers Johann André aus Offenbach sowie von Ferdinand Ries (Simrock, Bonn). August Eberhard Müller verfasste seinen Klavierauszug für Breitkopf & Härtel, der lt. Anzeige in der AMZ (30.7.1800) ebenfalls zu den frühzeitig erschienenen gehörte.

[22] Zit. nach Feder, *Die Schöpfung* (wie Anm. 13), S. 150.

[23] Brief Griesingers an Breitkopf vom 15.11.1800.

Afterword

Throughout his entire career, Joseph Haydn (1732-1809) placed the main focus of his creative work on instrumental music, with the burden falling on symphonies, string quartets, piano pieces, and chamber music. Nonetheless, he also tried his hand again and again at vocal works, albeit in much smaller quantity. Most if not all of these pieces were written for use in church. In 1782, however, Emperor Joseph II intervened high-handedly in the sovereignty of the ecclesiastical authorities and promulgated a divine ritual that largely banned festive music with instrumental accompaniment from the church. From then on, and specifically from 1783 to 1796, Haydn fell silent in this sector. It is a biographical miracle that when the emperor's decree was revoked the 64-year-old composer devoted almost the whole of his creative energies to choral music, producing large-scale new works that virtually added a new dimension to his already established fame. The years between 1796 and 1802 saw the emergence of the six great High Masses,[1] *The Seven Last Words of Our Savior on the Cross* (the vocal version was finished at the latest by early 1796), and the broadly-conceived oratorios, *The Creation* (1796-8) and *The Seasons* (completed in 1801). The latter two works, though not intended for use in church, were just as suitable as Handel's oratorios for performance in a sacred setting.

In the early 1790s, Haydn undertook two concert tours of England. After completing his highly successful second tour in 1795, he returned permanently to Vienna. He had never travelled far in his early years, having spent his busy life more or less between Vienna and Esterház, the country seat of his employer. Then in December 1790, at the age of nearly 58, he accepted one of several invitations from Johann Peter Salomon (1745-1816), a violinist and concert impresario resident in London from 1781, to conduct his own series of concerts in England. This possibility had only arisen with the death in September of his employer Prince Nicolaus I, the "Magnificent." His successor, Prince Anton, disbanded the Esterházy orchestra (retaining only the wind band for the hunt) and dismissed its director with a relatively modest pension.[2]

In this way Haydn quite suddenly entered a new and, for him, alien world. In London he experienced a public musical culture the likes of which were unknown in Vienna. The mere fact that five different subscription series were offered to a broad audience during his first season can only have left a lasting mark on him. He attended many concerts himself and was excited by the quality of the playing. His own concerts were brilliantly successful; indeed they were veritable triumphs that must have contributed hugely to his self-esteem. As a result, he undertook a second journey in 1794, again for two concert seasons. Once again, the success was great, and Haydn returned full of new impressions. Is it at all surprising that these experiences had a decisive impact on his future life and creative work?

Already during his first trip to England, in 1791, Haydn heard performances of Handel's oratorios in Westminster Abbey during the great Handel Commemoration Festival. The mighty sounds produced by the gigantic assembly of musicians left him astonished. In his own notes, Haydn reported that 885 people were said to be involved; other sources even mention a considerably greater number.[3] There can be no doubt that the event left a deep impression on the composer, and he probably soon lit on the idea of attempting a similar task himself, with Handel's *Messiah* as his yardstick. Tradition has it that Solomon gave him a libretto on the biblical creation myth that a man named Lidley was said to have written for Handel half a century earlier.[4] This libretto, based on John Milton's epic poem *Paradise Lost*, passed from Haydn to Baron Gottfried van Swieten (1733-1803), a prefect in the imperial court library in Vienna and the managing director of a society of aristocratic musical amateurs known as the "Association of Cavaliers."[5] Van Swieten gave the libretto a new twist, translating it into German and calling it *Die Schöpfung – The Creation*. "The proportion of my labors on the original English book exceeds, to be sure, that of a mere translation," he confided to the *Allgemeine Musikalische Zeitung*, "but it is far from being such that I could call the work my own."[6] Since Lidley's libretto, the basis of van Swieten's efforts, has not survived, the extent of the latter's involvement in the German translation has never been reliably determined. Moreover, several linguistic infelicities in the English quickly, and later repeatedly, provoked the suspicion that van Swieten placed his German translation text alongside, not the English original, but a self-made English retranslation of his own German version. In consequence, attempts were made to improve the language (at times with questionable results), which automatically entailed interventions in the musical diction. Today we know that van Swieten's command of English was insufficient to translate an entire libretto into what was, for him, a foreign language. But we also know that Haydn set a German libretto that van Swieten had extracted from the English text, at most enlarging it with a few additions from his own pen. Only at a later stage did he adapt the English text to the finished composition.[7] As a result, despite its shortcomings, we have largely retained this English version intact in our edition, apart from a few corrections listed in the critical commentary to the published score.[8]

But van Swieten functioned as more than a translator. In him Haydn found a comrade-in-arms whose free recasting of the original produced an effective libretto in the first place. Van Swieten also gave the composer pointed suggestions regarding the musical setting, suggestions that Haydn took thoroughly to heart. The precise fit of the words, to quote the composer in a different context, "simplifies the work of the composer, and the poet is compelled to write his words musically."[9] Finally, van Swieten and several noblemen friends – the "Associated Cavaliers" – agreed to underwrite the costs of the performance and provide Haydn with an appropriate honorarium. The fee was such as had never been paid to a composer before: 500 ducats, or five times what was usually paid at that time for an opera![10] The première performance was, accordingly, given in private surroundings before an audience of aristocrats and specially invited guests in the Viennese palace of Prince Schwarzenberg (demolished in 1893) on the New Market, or Neumarkt (now renamed Mehlmarkt). This event took place on 29 April 1798, and a repeat performance followed one day later. The first public performance had to wait a full year, when it was given in the old Burg Theater on 19 March 1799, Haydn's name day. Haydn conducted all these early performances himself. Many accounts by contemporary observers have survived, all of them unanimous in their view of its triumphant success: "The music has a power of representation that beggars the imagination; one is transported, one sees the clash of the elements, watches light flare into existence and the fallen spirits plunge into the abyss; one shudders at the peal of the thunder and sings along in the solemn hymn with the inhabitants of Paradise. The sun rises, the birds greet the morn with joyful praises; green tendrils spring from the soil, silvery waters babble in the cool brook, and Leviathan surges forth from the bottom of the sea on waves of foam. ... Three days have already passed since that happy evening, and the music still resounds in my ears [and] in my heart; the welter of sentiments continues to constrict my breast at the mere recollection."[11]

Haydn himself conducted several performances of *The Creation* until 1802 or 1803, even including one in Budapest (8 March 1800). Among them were the first private performances in the Schwarzenberg Palace in Vienna, several repeat performances at the same location that May and in March of the following year, the first public performances in the Burg Theater, and the concert initiated by the Vienna Tonkünstler-Sozietät (Society of Musicians) on 22-23 December 1799, likewise in the Burg Theater. All of these performances, provided that they were played from the original performance material, are especially important for a study of the sources and for the information they shed on performance practice.[12] Again and again Haydn made minor emendations, some of which he entered in the performance material, as we can see from his autograph annotations, and some of which he perhaps only transmitted orally, as several non-autograph annotations seem to suggest.

Haydn scholars have collected a large body of evidence on these early performances, and thus on the widely varying size of the orchestra and chorus.[13] It transpires that the work was given not only with minimum forces but with orchestras numbering up to some two-hundred musicians.[14]

It was Haydn's intention to publish the score himself rather than offering it to one of the Viennese publishers or, say, to Breitkopf & Härtel in Leipzig, despite the good contacts he maintained with the latter firm through their Viennese agent, the Saxon diplomat Georg August Griesinger (d. 1828). He therefore, in June 1799, published an invitation to subscribe in several leading newspapers: the *Wiener Zeitung* (17 June 1799) and the *Allgemeine Musikalische Zeitung* (26 June 1799, "Intelligenzblatt" no. xv). According to an advertisement from the publisher Artaria, who was entrusted with its marketing (*Wiener Zeitung*, 26 February 1800), the score was already available in print by the end of February 1800. Only after lengthy negotiations did Haydn finally sell the plates to Breitkopf & Härtel, Leipzig, in 1803. The score was issued many times from these plates with the name of the new publisher until 1871, when it became necessary to have the work re-engraved. That plates frequently had to be re-engraved due to wear and tear is not only self-evident but also well-documented.

For many years the original print issued by Haydn himself served as a production master for later prints from various publishers, including the newly engraved version issued by C. F. Peters in 1871.[15] The preface to that edition mentions several changes made to the original master, but it also includes, without comment, sundry "improvements" undertaken in the spirit of the time. In particular, this involved the addition of articulation marks, with the result that presumably intentional inconsistencies in parallel passages in the original were ironed out.

Our new edition attaches great importance to Haydn's original print, particularly as the composer not only vetted the engraver's copy, as is proved by his autograph markings, but also probably read proof, since there are several changes *vis-à-vis* the engraver's copy that can hardly have originated with the other persons involved, such as van Swieten or even the engraver.

Although Haydn sanctioned the work's tripartite division, he did not number its individual movements. As a result, the original print likewise appeared without numbers. A continuous enumeration to 34 was entered in the engraver's copy, presumably at a much later date. This enumeration is identical to the one in the old Peter's score, and was probably even taken from that print. Later generations have tried again and again to introduce a numbering system of their own, with highly conflicting results. Proceeding from the numbering system in the old Peters edition – and ignoring several conflicting subdivisions of the movements – we have retained the earlier Peters numbers with only one exception: Raphael's recitative ("Im Anfange schuf Gott Himmel und Erde") has been extracted from no. 1 and listed independently as no. 2. In this case we have followed the precedent of Eusebius Mandyczewski when he edited the volume for the old Haydn complete edition (Breitkopf & Härtel, 1924).[16] As a result, our new edition has 35 numbers.[17]

Performances of Haydn's late vocal works constantly raise the question of the need for non-notated embellishments, i.e. ornaments and melismas. Haydn is known to have looked askance at the willfulness of singers.[18] Nonetheless, as we know from Albert Christoph Dies's account of the performance of *The Creation* in March 1808 (Haydn's last appearance in public), he found words of praise for the soprano Therese Fischer: "she sang her part with maximum delicacy, and with such fidelity that she did not allow herself the least inappropriate addition."[19] From this we can conclude with some certainty that Haydn had no objection to suitable embellishments when properly executed. Indeed, the set of parts used at the première and other material from Haydn's posthumous estate contain various alternative embellishments for the soloists. As their date of origin is uncertain, we may safely assume that they only entered the manuscripts at some later time and that Haydn was unaware of them. All the same, they provide some evidence for an established line of tradition and have therefore been incorporated in our edition in small print as suggestions that performers are at liberty to use with all due caution.

As a rule, Haydn himself only employed four ornamentation symbols: the standard trill sign (*tr*), the sign for an inverted mordent (∾), the so-called turn or "gruppetto" (∞), and a sign which he himself referred to as a "half-mordent" (⸸).[20] Still, the sources confront us with many ambiguities regarding the proper representation of the ornament concerned. We have attempted wherever possible to maintain these distinctions and to incorporate them in our new edition.

This volume adheres to the standards of modern editorial practice. Special attention has been given to the notation of appoggiaturas. The editor has decided in favor of the so-called "halved note-value notation," even departing from the sources where necessary. Haydn himself followed this practice at times, albeit none too consistently in his later years, when he frequently wrote appoggiaturas as eighth notes regardless of the value of the principal note. In our new edition, however, we have retained the sixteenth-note as the smallest unit for appoggiaturas, even when they happen to precede sixteenths or lesser note values, and regardless of whether they are meant to be played long or short.

As far as articulation marks are concerned, we have followed the findings in each principal source. Great importance was attached to the distinction between dots and strokes to indicate staccato (the latter occasionally have a double meaning and readily permit an interpretation as accent marks). Questionable or completely contradictory readings are discussed in the editorial comments in the printed score. We have been very sparing in our use of editorial additions and have refrained from mindless standardization so as to avoid the danger of blandness. As a result, performers are granted sufficient leeway for their own interpretations, particularly as the existing articulation marks very often indicate nothing more than one line and do not always need to be consistently maintained.

In many details the present vocal score has taken as its guide the old edition of 1800 by August Eberhard Müller (1767-1817), but without adopting it *in toto*. This vocal score, prepared by the cantor of the Leipzig Thomaskirche (1804-10) and later conductor at the Viennese court, was one of four competing editions published in rapid succession within that same year.[21] Another vocal score was announced in Vienna by Mollo in 1799 even before the full score of *The Creation* had appeared in print. Haydn is said to have been very annoyed at it and called it a "wretched piece of patchwork".[22] Müller's vocal score, on the other, received high commendation from none other than Haydn himself, who called it "the best, most intelligible, and easiest among its brethren."[23]

Klaus Burmeister

---

[1] These are the *Missa in tempore belli* ("Kettledrum Mass," Hob. XXII: 9), the *Heiligmesse* ("Holy Mass," no. 10), the *Missa in angustiis* ("Nelson Mass," no. 11), the *Theresienmesse* ("Theresa Mass," no. 12), the *Schöpfungsmesse* ("Creation Mass," no. 13), and the *Harmoniemesse* ("Wind Band Mass," no. 14). Haydn was commissioned to write these works by his final employer, Nicolaus II, who intended them to be a gift for the name-day festivities of his wife, Josepha Hermenegild.

[2] After Prince Anton's death on 22 January 1794 his son, Nicolaus II, summoned Haydn to return from his second tour of England, to reassemble the orchestra, and to assume its nominal leadership with the task, among other things, of composing one Mass every year (see note 1).

[3] Haydn wrote the number "885" in his two so-called London Notebooks; see Dénes Bartha, ed.: *Joseph Haydn: Gesammelte Briefe und Aufzeichnungen* (Kassel, 1965), pp. 485 and 506. C. F. Pohl, on page 136 of his *Haydn in London* (Vienna, 1867), puts this figure at more than one thousand.

[4] Georg August Griesinger: *Biographische Notizen über Joseph Haydn* (Leipzig, 1810: repr. Leipzig, 1975), p. 51. The name Lidley mentioned by Griesinger is not verified in any other source. Although various writers have been taken into consideration over the years, the authorship of the English libretto has remained unclear to the present day. Textual comparisons have revealed that the English original derives at least from one strand in the *Paradise Lost* tradition.

[5] These "associated cavaliers," as Haydn refers to them in a letter of 3 July 1801 to Griesinger (Bartha, see note 3, pp. 368f.), constituted "a society of friends of music ... which consisted of a small number of members and was wont to put on several academies each year" (translated from Griesinger's report in the *Allgemeine Musikalische Zeitung* of 20 May 1801, which mentions the names "*Lichtenstein, Esterhazy, Schwarzenberg, Auersperg, Lobkowitz, Lichnowsky, Trautmannsdorf, Swieten, Czernin, Fries, Aponi, Sinzendorf, Kinsky, Erdödy [and] Harrach*"). The "cavaliers" had been mounting and financing performances of large-scale vocal music since 1786, including works by J. A. Hasse, C. Ph. E. Bach, and Handel in the wellknown arrangements by Mozart.

[6] Translated from van Swieten's letter published in *Allgemeine Musikalische Zeitung*, i, no. 16 (3 January 1799).

[7] See Nicholas Temperley: "New Light on the Libretto of The Creation," *Music in Eighteenth-Century England*, ed. by Christopher Hogwood and Richard Luckett (Cambridge, 1983), pp. 189-211.

[8] The English version of the text is not included in the original performance material, but it has survived in a handwritten score deriving from Haydn's posthumous estate (presently located in the Staatsbibliothek Preussischer Kulturbesitz, Berlin) as well as the engraver's copy and Haydn's original print. For a detailed source description see the critical comments in the score edition.

[9] Letter of 21 April 1802 by Griesinger, translated from Günter Thomas, ed.: "Griesingers Briefe über Haydn," *Haydn-Studien*, i/2 (Munich and Duisburg, 1966), p. 89.

[10] 500 ducats were equivalent to 2250 gulden. To appreciate the value of this amount we need only compare it to the annual salary of a schoolteacher at that time (at most 250 gulden) or to Haydn's own annual salary as conductor of the Esterházy orchestra (1700 gulden in 1797).

[11] Quoted from a report of 3 May 1798, presumably written by Friedrich Joseph Ritter von Retzer, and published in *Der neue Teutsche Merkur*, ed. by C. M. Wieland (Weimar, 1798), item 6, June 1798, vol. ii, p. 190.

[12] The material used by Haydn in his own performances (a copyists' manuscript in score and a set of handwritten parts) passed from the holdings of the Vienna Tonkünstler-Sozietät to the Vienna City and State Library. They are among the sources consulted for our new edition.

[13] See A. Peter Brown: *Performing Haydn's The Creation: Reconstruction of the Earliest Renditions* (Bloomington, Ind., 1986) and Georg Feder: *Joseph Haydn: Die Schöpfung* (Kassel, 1999).

[14] Haydn himself considered anything other than large forces unsuitable: "My composition is writ large, he said, and will thus only be content and achieve its due effect with a large and well-trained orchestra." Thus Griesinger's letter of 5 February 1800 to Breitkopf & Härtel, quoted in Otto Biba: "*Eben komme ich von Haydn...*": *Georg August Griesingers Korrespondenz mit Joseph Haydns Verleger Breitkopf & Härtel 1799-1819* (Zurich, 1987).

[15] Publisher's number EP 1029, plate number 5453.

[16] *Joseph Haydns Werke: Erste kritisch durchgesehene Gesamtausgabe*, series 16: *Kantaten und Oratorien*, vol. v: *Die Schöpfung*, with a preface and editorial notes by E. Mandyczewski (Leipzig: Breitkopf & Härtel, 1924). This volume, based on the original edition but with only the German text, also appeared in Breitkopf & Härtel's library of scores (no. 4381).

[17] Owing to its different subdivisions, the Breitkopf editions stop at no. 32.

[18] Haydn's biographer Giuseppe Carpani even maintained that the solo parts should be "performed with simplicity, accuracy, expression, and portamento, but without embellishment." See *Le Haydine ovvero lettre su la vita e le opere del celebre maestro Giuseppe Haydn* (Milan, 1812), p. 182.

[19] Albert Christoph Dies: *Biographische Nachrichten von Joseph Haydn* (Vienna, 1810); new edition by Horst Seeger (Berlin, 1959, ⁴1976), p. 175.

[20] Haydn presented these four "musical signs" in a letter of 20 July 1781 to Artaria and expressly referred to the "half-mordent" in a letter of 10 December 1785 to the same publisher. See Bartha (note 3), pp. 101 and 148.

[21] The other vocal scores of 1800 stem from Haydn's pupil Sigismund Ritter von Neukomm (Vienna: Artaria), Anton André, the son and successor of the once well-known music publisher Johann André (Offenbach), and Ferdinand Ries (Bonn: Simrock). August Eberhard Müller prepared his vocal score for Breitkopf & Härtel. An advertisement in the *Allgemeine Musikalische Zeitung* (30 July 1800) reveals that it, too, was among the first ones to appear.

[22] Translated from Feder: *Die Schöpfung* (see note 13), p. 150.

[23] Griesinger's letter of 15 November 1800 to Breitkopf.

CHORSINGEN – LEICHT GEMACHT

JOHANN SEBASTIAN BACH
- Johannes-Passion BWV 245
  Klavierauszug EP 8635
  CD: MPC 8635-1/2/3/4 (je 2 CDs)
- Matthäus-Passion BWV 244
  Klavierauszug EP 4503
  CD: MPC 4503-1/2/3/4 (je 2 CDs)
- Messe h-Moll BWV 232
  Klavierauszug EP 8736
  CD für S1 / S2 / A / T / B:
  MPC 8736-11/12/2/3/4 (je 2 CDs)
- Weihnachtsoratorium BWV 248
  Klavierauszug EP 8719
  CD: MPC 8719-1/2/3/4 (je 2 CDs)

LUDWIG VAN BEETHOVEN
- 9. Symphonie / Chorfantasie c-Moll
  Klavierauszug 9. Symphonie EP 2227
  Klavierauszug Chorfantasie EP 8723
  CD: MPC 8723-1/2/3/4

JOHANNES BRAHMS
- Ein deutsches Requiem op. 45
  Klavierauszug EP 3672
  CD: MPC 3672-1/2/3/4 (je 2 CDs)

ANTONÍN DVOŘÁK
- Stabat Mater op. 58
  Klavierauszug EP 8639
  CD: MPC 8639-1/2/3/4 (je 2 CDs)

GABRIEL FAURÉ
- Requiem op. 48
  Klavierauszug EP 9562
  CD: MPC 9562-1/2/3/4

CHARLES GOUNOD
- Messe solennelle G-Dur (Cäcilienmesse)
  Klavierauszug EP 8729
  CD: MPC 8729-1/2/3/4

GEORG FRIEDRICH HÄNDEL
- Der Messias HWV 56
  (auf CD gesungen in deutsch)
  Klavierauszug EP 4501
  CD: MPC 4501-1/2/3/4 (je 2 CDs)

MPC Nr.: 1/2/3/4: 1=Sopran; 2=Alt; 3=Tenor; 4=Bass

JOSEPH HAYDN
- Die Schöpfung Hob. XXI: 2
  Klavierauszug EP 8998
  CD: MPC 66-1/2/3/4
- Die Jahreszeiten Hob. XXI: 3
  Klavierauszug EP 11031
  CD: MPC 11031-1/2/3/4

FELIX MENDELSSOHN BARTHOLDY
- Elias op. 70
  Klavierauszug EP 1749
  CD: MPC 1749-1/2/3/4 (je 2 CDs)
- 2. Symphonie (Lobgesang) B-Dur op. 52
  Klavierauszug EP 1750
  CD: MPC 1750-1/2/3/4
- Die erste Walpurgisnacht op. 60
  Klavierauszug EP 1752
  CD: MPC 1752-1/2/3/4
- Paulus op. 36
  Klavierauszug EP 1748
  CD: MPC 1748-1/2/3/4

WOLFGANG AMADEUS MOZART
- Missa C-Dur KV 317 (Krönungsmesse)
  Klavierauszug EP 8115
  CD: MPC 8115-1/2/3/4
- Requiem d-Moll KV 626 (Beyer)
  Klavierauszug EP 8700a
  CD: MPC 8700-1/2/3/4
- Missa c-Moll KV 427
  Klavierauszug EP 8706
  CD: MPC 8706-1/2/3/4

GIOACCHINO ROSSINI
- Petite Messe solennelle
  Partitur (=Klavierauszug) EP 8684
  CD: MPC 8684-1/2/3/4

FRANZ SCHUBERT
- Messe G-Dur D 167
  Klavierauszug EP 10858
  CD: MPC 1049-1/2/3/4

GIUSEPPE VERDI
- Requiem
  Klavierauszug EP 4251
  CD: MPC 4251-1/2/3/4 (je 2 CDs)

C. F. Peters · Frankfurt/M. · Leipzig · London · New York
www.edition-peters.de